TechnoBrands

TechnoBrands

HOW TO CREATE & USE "BRAND IDENTITY" TO MARKET, ADVERTISE & SELL TECHNOLOGY PRODUCTS

Chuck Pettis

American Management Association

New York ● Atlanta ● Boston ● Chicago ● Kansas City ● San Francisco ● Washington, D.C.
Brussels ● Mexico City ● Tokyo ● Toronto

Library of Congress Cataloging-in-Publication Data

Pettis, Chuck, 1948–
    TechnoBrands : how to create & use "brand identity" to market,
advertise & sell technology products / Chuck Pettis.
    p. cm.
Includes bibliographical references and index.
ISBN 0-8144-0243-7
    1. High technology—Marketing.   2. Technological innovations—
Marketing.   3. Brand name products.   I. Title.
HC79.H53P48   1995
620'.006'8—dc20   94-31044
                                                CIP

TechnoBrands and TechnoBranding are servicemarks of Floathe
Johnson Associates, Inc., Kirkland, WA. Telephone: 206-822-8400.

Printing number

10 9 8 7 6 5 4 3 2 1

To my parents, who have always given me the freedom and support to think outside the lines.

To my sons, who asked for something I could pass on to them.

Contents

4 The TechnoBranding Process   54

*The Changing Role of Branding in High-Tech • Small
Is TechnoWonderful • TechnoBranding: The Six Basic
Steps to Build a Strong TechnoBrand • Tips for Small
and Medium-Sized Companies • Start Today • The
Intel Brand Campaign • How Does TechnoBranding
Get Results? • How Much Is Enough? • Adopt
TechnoBrand Management*

5 The Absolute Importance of Research   81

*Know the Customer • Start with What You Can Afford
• Ask Questions before Beginning • Primary
Qualitative and Quantitative Research
• TechnoBranding Qualitative Study • TechnoBranding
Quantitative Study • Ongoing Brand Tracking*

6 Defining the Brand   106

*The Positioning Statement • Brand Associations
• Nodal Maps • Brand Ladders • The Applied
Microsystems Frog Campaign*

**7 Integrating Brand Strategy and Marketing
Communications**   136

*Integrated Marketing Communications • Benefits of
Integrated Marketing Communications • IMC Tools
• Brand Advertising: The Good, the Bad, and the Ugly
• Packaging Sells • Public Relations and Direct
Marketing • A Model for Building Brand, One Step at
a Time • Evaluating TechnoBrand Creative • The
Emerging Revolution in Interactive Media • Using
Timing to Your Advantage • Charisma*

8 Creatively Implementing TechnoBranding   165

*Which Comes First, Brand or Corporate Culture?
• Institutionalizing Brand at FWB • TechnoBranding
Service Businesses • What's in a Name? • What's in a
Logo? • Company Brand versus Product • Brand
Extension • Brand Name, Research, and Extension at
Microsoft • Organizing for Brand Management*

Preface And Acknowledgments

I believe in the power of collaboration and the power of teams. This book wouldn't exist without the combined efforts of many people who care deeply about the art, craft, and science of Techno-Branding.

TechnoBranding got started in 1991 when I decided that Floathe Johnson, a high-tech advertising and public relations agency, needed something to differentiate it from other agencies. "High-tech" had differentiated us in the 1980s, when a high-tech agency stood out, but not in the 1990s, when all agencies are moving in on the action in high-tech. We needed to start practicing what we were preaching to clients: Find your point of differentiation and build a brand with it.

We did focus groups of prospective clients in Seattle, Portland, and San Francisco. We found that high-tech marketers agreed with us: Companies that don't build their brands are putting themselves at risk. But most marketers didn't have an in-depth understanding of how to actually manage brands.

A group of us working at the agency decided to explore how brand marketing could not only differentiate our agency, but help us improve the quality of our creative work as well. That group included John Engerman, Ann Demitruk, Joe LePla, Terry Short, Neil Stewart, Greg Weber, and Lynn Parker, supported by the Floathe Johnson management team: Maury Floathe, Greg Johnson, Katherine James Schuitemaker, Dick Simmons, and Jim Rose. Actually, everyone in the agency has helped. "You know who you are."

The term *TechnoBranding* was coined by Neil Stewart, a London-based account planner dedicated to technology markets, when he spent several months working at Floathe Johnson in Kirkland, Washington. He got up in front of the group one day and presented TechnoBranding as a Hegelian dialectic! (See the beginning of Chapter 8 for his presentation.) Neil has contributed significantly to this book by providing much background reading and many original comments and ideas, including the new marketing paradigm in Chapter 2.

Lynn Parker played a major role in developing the TechnoBranding process. Joe LePla introduced nodal maps. Thanks to Joe and Stoel Rives for material on building brand with investors. Dick Simmons contributed, creatively. The public relations group helped with papers and articles.

Through it all, Maury Floathe and Greg Johnson have supported this R&D effort to help build a great agency. Thank you, Maury, for permission to use copyrighted materials. Katherine James Schuitemaker, now with Aldus, was instrumental in developing, refining, and proving the TechnoBranding concepts. Dan Bockman's continual questioning—"Now, Chuck, I still don't get TechnoBranding"—helped push the edge further out.

My writing partners have been Evelyn Clark, corporate storyteller, and David McCreary, writer and direct marketer. Evelyn helped me with many of the interviews in the book, adding the depth of real-life experiences with brands. David added a level of organization, flow, and consistent style that were sorely needed. Both have helped with heavy editing. A great time has been had.

All quotations, unless otherwise indicated, come from personal interviews and are used with permission. Larry Light was kind enough to give permission to use not only his quotations, but many of his terms (e.g., demarketing) and ideas as well.

The charts from IDG, Techtel, and Geoffrey Moore; the Intel, Microsoft, and Applied Microsystems advertisements; and the Heart Interface nodal map and brand ladder are all used by permission.

The following people helped by reviewing the manuscript and providing comments, contributions, and editing suggestions: Peter Raulerson, Rosemary Newman, Neil Stewart, Claudia Jacob, Joe LePla, Lynn Parker, Suzette Cavanaugh, and Mike Kelly. Thanks to Faye Bickle and everyone else who helped.

Thanks to Noreen Brownlie, who led me to my wonderful agent, Linda Allen. Thank you to Adrienne Hickey, Jacqueline Laks Gorman, and the rest of the AMACOM staff, who showed me the real added value a publisher provides to its authors.

Finally, special thanks to Floathe Johnson TechnoBranding clients and all the people who shared their branding knowledge and experience: John Ardussi, Ira Bachrach, Arthur W. Buerk, Skip Cavanaugh, Kelly Conlin, Mark Craemer, Steve Dearden, Arthur Einstein, Jerry Gibbons, Steve Goodman, Robin Harper, Peter Horan, George Hubman, Mike Isaacson, Michael Kelly, John Konsin, Derrith Lambka, Norm Levy, Larry Light, Wendy Lung, Helen Manich, Chris McAndrews, Patrick J. McGovern, Geoffrey Moore, Bill Mowry, Sally Narodick, Ken Needham, John O'Toole, C. E. "Charlie" Pankenier, Robert Ratliffe, Peter Raulerson, Dave Roberts, Ken Rutsky, Maurice Schafer, Brian Sharples, Heidi Sinclair, Warren Stokes, Dave Sutherland, Marty Taucher, Vanessa Torres, Debra Triant, Rod Turner, Roy Verley, Teri Wiegman, Floyd Willison, plus all the other people referenced directly or indirectly herein.

C. P.

TechnoBrands

Introduction

For many years, technology marketers could build a better mousetrap (or mouse), then sit back and watch the customers, money in hand, line up at their door. Those days are gone. In the face of global competition, downsizing, and mature markets, even the best mousetrap no longer guarantees success.

In a world demanding increased "compatibility," technology for its own sake is no longer an adequate product differential. Better brand identity and customer-oriented benefits, not better specifications, will determine who remains in business. Yet, many technology executives and marketers continue to regard brand as something that belongs on a supermarket shelf.

A major story on brands appears in the news almost every week. From the covers of *Fortune* to *Advertising Age* to *American Demographics*, the business world appears to be rediscovering brand values, while beneath the headlines a battle rages—a battle for market share, sales, and market dominance. It's the battle of the brands, it's a fight to the finish, and too many high-technology executives don't even know it exists. Even worse, they don't realize that their competitors, blatantly using brand advertising, are digging their foundations out from under them.

The market has radically changed. The rules have changed. The one stable factor is ignorance.

The few companies who possess the "secrets" of brand marketing have a decided business advantage. Major technology companies that fail to build their brands won't be able to catch up. Smaller companies will go out of business or be forced to merge or sell out.

Where can today's busy technology brand managers and marketing communications providers find the help they desperately need? Available books on branding talk almost exclusively about consumer brands. Even then they talk in generalities and theory. What help is there for companies and executives who want to understand what is going on and what they must do to fight back and win? Until *TechnoBrands*, not much.

TechnoBrands capitalizes on the increasing thirst for brand information evidenced in the news, and the complete lack of information on how to build brands for technology products.

TechnoBrands talks in practical engineering and manufacturing language—"What will it do for me?" and "How do I do it?" Here are some of the real marketing questions TechnoBranding can answer:

- How do you pick and develop a brand name?
- What's more important, the company brand or the product brand?
- How do you brand services?
- How do you build a brand with a limited budget?
- How can you find the optimal premium price you can charge for your brand?
- What's the role of brand with the distribution channel?
- How do you extend and leverage your brand name?
- How can you "transcreate" brands internationally?
- How do you build brand equity and increase perceived value, quality, and customer satisfaction?

To understand what's happening in high-tech markets today, let's go back to the person who first marketed soap. He had the market to himself—until a competitor came along and added some perfume to the formula. Then another competitor added a little dye. Soon there were many soaps that looked and smelled alike; people were confused.

Next, someone had the idea of associating his soap with a certain image or attribute that distinguished it from other soaps. In time, when people thought of soap, they also thought of children, fruit, Dutch women, bright packaging, or catchy names and tag lines like "It floats!" Then one day, manufacturers discovered that those images were just as important as the products. Sometimes they were even more important.

HP, Apple, IBM, Microsoft. Obviously, brand associations work for technology products as well as for consumer products. However, before you begin printing three-masted sailing ships on PC boards, there's an important fact to remember: Technology buyers are different from the buyers of consumer products. That doesn't mean that they go home at night, step out of their human skins, and become lizards from outer space. Rather, it means that they buy technology products differently from the way they buy soap.

If you don't like the shampoo you bought last week, you buy another shampoo this week. If you don't like the $50,000 network upgrade you bought last week—oops! Successful technology buyers become information junkies because a wrong decision costs a lot of money (or even a job). Therefore, when they buy a product, they ask lots of questions, and the two they ask most often are:

1. Will this product do what we need?
2. Can we depend on the company that sells it?

In order for your customers to be able to answer yes to these questions, they need to know who you are, know what you make, believe in your solution, and trust you. The process Floathe Johnson has developed for enabling your customers to do this is called TechnoBranding.

TechnoBranding codifies a modern, technological approach to branding. It takes the best in theory and practice from the world of consumer branding and blends them into a coherent, proven system that can be applied to the branding of technology-based products. It is designed for use in the real world. TechnoBranding is a systematic way for companies to not only gain competitive advantage but become a dominant force in the marketplace, because branding has not been widely practiced by technology companies.

TechnoBrands is for managers and marketers of all technology-based products. It is also for the layperson who wants to know more about the influence of brands on his or her own purchases and for the nontechnology businessperson who can directly apply the principles herein to his or her own business, whether it be a small retail shop or a service business. In short, *TechnoBrands* illuminates the mystique of brands.

Although most technology-based products today are sold to businesses, more and more technological products, such as computers, telecommunications, office equipment, and, of course, consumer electronics, are entering the mass market and being sold directly to knowledgeable consumers.

As you know, today's technology buyers are smart. Your communications need to deliver meaningful data that they can access quickly. They want that data presented in their language, and they expect you to understand both their technology and their business.

Unless you have just invented a new technology, you have competitors. Their products may not perform exactly like yours; however, to the busy technology buyer, bombarded daily by thousands of sales messages, you and your competitors look pretty much alike. Brand, then, lets you differentiate your product from its competition.

Brand building is important to small and medium-sized companies, not just those companies that are household names. You'll find that the techniques explained in *TechnoBrands* apply to small as well as large companies. Also, *TechnoBrands* does not apply only to computer companies, even though most of the examples used in the book are from the computer industry. That's because brand is a hot issue in computer and software marketing today and examples are readily available. The principles apply equally well and the same level of urgency exists for all technology companies.

The purpose of *TechnoBrands* is sixfold:

1. To educate businesspeople and students about the importance of brand to technology companies (Chapters 1 and 4)
2. To examine the changes in technology market dynamics that make brand building imperative for corporate survival and health (Chapter 2)
3. To differentiate between consumer and technology brand building (Chapter 3)
4. To lay out the TechnoBranding steps and techniques so that you can research, define, develop, and apply brand to your

company's products through all customer relationships (Chapters 4, 5, 6, 7, and 8)
5. To explain the importance of and techniques for using brands internationally (Chapter 9)
6. To explain the bottom-line benefits of building brand equity (Chapter 10)

The TechnoBranding process is as important as the advances we've seen in technology itself. Discover the power of the brand before it's too late. If you put the lessons of this book into effect, then the success of your company will be assured in the years to come.

1

What Is a Brand And Why Is It Important?

"Buildings age and become dilapidated.
Machines wear out.
People die.
But what live on are the brands."

Sir Hector Laing,
Group Chief Executive of Britain's United Biscuits[1]

"The concept of brand is probably the most powerful idea in the commercial world."

Don Cowley, *Understanding Brands*[2]

"People will ask what's wrong with your product if you don't put your name on it."

Gian Carlo Bisone,
Compaq marketing vice president[3]

What you buy when you go to a car dealership is more than a collection of metal and plastic parts. You probably arrived at that particular dealer because of associations you have with a certain "brand." If you are at a Volvo dealership, the association "safety" influences you to contemplate purchase; if you are at a Honda dealership, the association "reliability" helps you make your decision; if "buy American" is a strong motivator, you may end up at a Chrysler or Saturn dealer. Each brand has a personality, an image, a set of associations that brought you there. On the other side of the coin, people will buy the product because of what it says about them. "I will buy Volvo because I want people to think I'm safety conscious, although I am not really."

Whether it's a technical product or a consumer product, branding is very important. Many technical products are closer to consumer products than most people would like to believe.

A brand becomes an asset over a period of time. Like a seedling, it takes constant care and frequent watering to produce a flower. Brand equity doesn't just happen; it's a combination of quality product, advertising, marketing programs, point-of-sale programs, customer-service programs—a bundle of customer experiences that create the ultimate brand image.

Brand Defined

What exactly is a brand? A brand is:

- The sensory, emotive, and cultural proprietary image surrounding a company or product
- An assurance of quality, making selection worry-free
- A significant source of competitive advantage and future earnings
- A promise of performance
- An enhancement of perceived value and satisfaction through associations that remind and entice customers to use the product
- Arguably, a company's most important asset

Branding goes back to the beginnings of history, when people began putting symbols on products to identify the maker of the product. From ancient Egyptian bricks to trade guilds in medieval Europe, people have been using "trademarks" on their products as a guarantee to customers of authenticity and quality and to protect their products from being copied by others.

The first appearance of brand names was in the early sixteenth century. To distinguish their whiskey from competitors' and to prevent tavern owners from substituting cheaper products, whiskey distillers burned or "branded" their name on the top of each barrel.[4]

The word *brand* is derived from "to burn"; hence the branding iron of the American West. In the cattle business, ownership is everything, and brand is the key to ownership. Ranches were named after their brands, and, as symbols, the brands were held in as high a regard as knights' crests or a nation's flag. For ranchers, the brand said "hands off." Today, branded products say "hands on."[5]

Using Branding to Get a Premium Price for Oranges

"Branding is one of the major strengths and purposes of advertising," according to John O'Toole, past president of the American Association of Advertising Agencies (A.A.A.A.). O'Toole spent thirty-two years with an agency that had handled the Sunkist Growers account since 1908. He calls it "the purest example of branding in my experience."

As O'Toole explains it, from the very beginning, Sunkist's purpose, whether stated or not, was to produce a branded agricultural product. It found a way of stamping the Sunkist logo on every one of the oranges that Sunkist produced and marketed—in effect, putting a package around them. And Sunkist created an advertising campaign to establish the superiority of these oranges over others that didn't bear the stamp.

"The benefit for the Sunkist Growers is the premium price consumers will pay for an orange with that Sunkist stamp, which at one time was around fifteen cents for every dollar," O'Toole says.

To command that kind of premium price, the product has to live up to the quality promised in the advertising. O'Toole says the Sunkist product surpassed the promise.

The Mind Game of Branding

Brands become storehouses of the words, feelings, and meanings that customers not only associate with the brand, but also use to define themselves in an ever-changing society. One common definition of brand is the summary of a customer's expectations of a company or line of products. It's all the values that they expect when they make a buying decision—over and above the product.

Brands stand as comfort anchors in the sea of confusion, fear, and doubt. Once customers have made a decision about a brand and its associations, they can be exceptionally loyal to that brand, continuing to buy it in the future, recommending it to friends, and choosing the product over others, even those with better feature sets or lower prices.

Arthur Einstein, a New York–based consultant who coordinated IBM's 1993 advertising agency review, defines brands as "nothing but shorthand for the consumer. Consumers use this shorthand to resolve conflicts and confusion as they cope with the vast and growing number of choices the market offers."[6] Which should I buy? Where should I buy? Whom can I depend on? Whom can I trust? Brand traits and brand character help to answer these questions.

"What exactly are brands made of?" Einstein asks. "They're existential; that is, nothing more (or less) than the sum total of how the maker behaves, the character and features of what it makes, sells, or services, and how these qualities come together and fit into a market context."

While a product can be touched and felt, the brand itself is not a tangible thing. It is an abstraction.

"Branding is a mind game," Einstein asserts. He adds that in dynamic markets, brands become fluid—not necessarily because they've changed, but because new competitors, new attitudes, and new expectations change the context in which a brand plays.

Einstein uses the Intel, Microsoft, IBM brand triangle to show how brand fluidity in a dynamic market creates a marketing tug-of-war. Intel, Microsoft, and IBM each want the consumer to believe that theirs is the brand to depend on for satisfaction in a PC purchase. Intel says the processor makes the difference. Microsoft says it's the software. IBM says it's the way the system is put together. Each claim has some truth to it, but today, neither the processor, the software, nor the system is unique or irreplaceable. In a situation such as this, the channel, which is a brand in its own right (Macy's, Sears, CompUSA), may enter into the purchase decision and become the factor that swings that decision one way or another.

Fluidity also implies continual change. A brand needs watching and rejuvenation to keep it current and of value to the consumer if it is not to become a commodity.

This investment is worth it because in dynamic markets, strong brands have more value than ever, precisely because of the speed with which these markets move. Bombarded with competing products, conflicting claims, and a more complex market environment, consumers need brands they can trust now more than ever. But consumers are also better educated and more skeptical than ever. "So brands that earn their trust and back them up are winners," Einstein says. "Those that fail them are Chapter 11 candidates."

Empirical Research on the Importance of Branding

"Branding has become much more important recently because of the proliferation of choice that's available to customers," according to Patrick J. McGovern, chairman of the board of International Data Group (IDG), the world's largest computer publishing and research company. McGovern ought to know—he started IDG in 1964, when the leading computer brands included Sperry-Univac, Burroughs, and, of course, IBM. "What's been fascinating to watch over the last thirty years is technology marketers 'discovering' the value of brand marketing only later in the product's life cycle," McGovern continues. "Technologists tend to think that technology alone will sell their product—that superior technology is the only thing that differentiates them from their competitors. In fact, customers, especially now that the PC market has exploded the product choices available, are anxious to feel secure in their product purchase, and brand image—by conveying the commitment of the vendor to the product and its service and support—plays a key role in providing that security."

IDG does extensive research on this topic. It has initiated a series of studies called "Buying I.T. (Information Technology) in the '90s" that explores the relationship between computer buyers and their brand decision, among other things. In late 1992, IDG explored the relative importance of brand, price, and distribution channel for corporate buyers of computer products. In a survey of

947 buyers conducted for IDG by IntelliQuest, respondents identified the most important factor driving the selection of desktop PCs, notebook PCs, printers, application software, and local area networks (LANs). As seen in Figure 1-1, the most important factor is brand.

So, brand matters a great deal, but how *many* brands do computer buyers consider? The IDG research indicates that for a typical purchase, very few. On average, participants in the survey reported that they considered just 2.7 notebook PC brands prior to their last purchase—and that is the high end for the categories studied. For printers and LANs, this figure drops to only 1.9 brands.[7]

Subsequent IDG research in 1993 supports these findings while providing more product detail. For example, as seen in Figure 1-2, for application software and network operating systems software, the percentage of corporate buyers who considered only one or two brands prior to their last purchase is consistently high.

In short, the *consideration set* of brands for computer product purchases is very small.

Price differentials, product displays, or point-of-purchase advertising may expand the consideration set a buyer had formed before she entered the channel of distribution. However, IDG's research demonstrates that the odds are heavily against a brand first considered when the buyer is actively shopping. Approximately 80 percent of the respondents in the "channels" study selected a brand they had considered *before* entering the channel. Even for desktop PCs, which many have described as a price-driven item, 77 percent left the "store" with a brand from their prechannel consideration set.[8]

For a vendor, then, the challenge is to generate buyer consideration of its brand early in the purchase process rather than hoping to catch the buyer's eye at the point of purchase. The best predictor of consideration is unaided brand awareness. Generally speaking, if two people are aware of a brand without prompting, one of the two will include that brand in his consideration set.[9]

How can a vendor build the brand awareness that leads to consideration? To answer this question, IDG asked corporate buyers in the "channels" survey which sources they used to gain information about the five product categories studied. The top two

(*text continues on page 14*)

Figure 1-1. Most important factor when purchasing product.

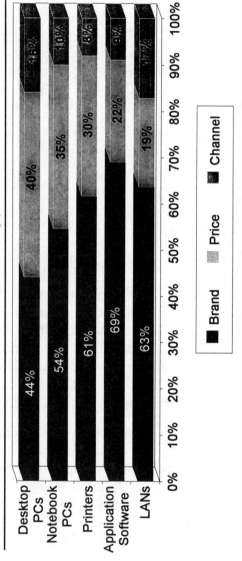

Source: International Data Group, "Buying I.T. in the '90s: The Channels," Boston, 1992, p. 85.

Figure 1-2. Number of brands considered prior to last purchase (business).

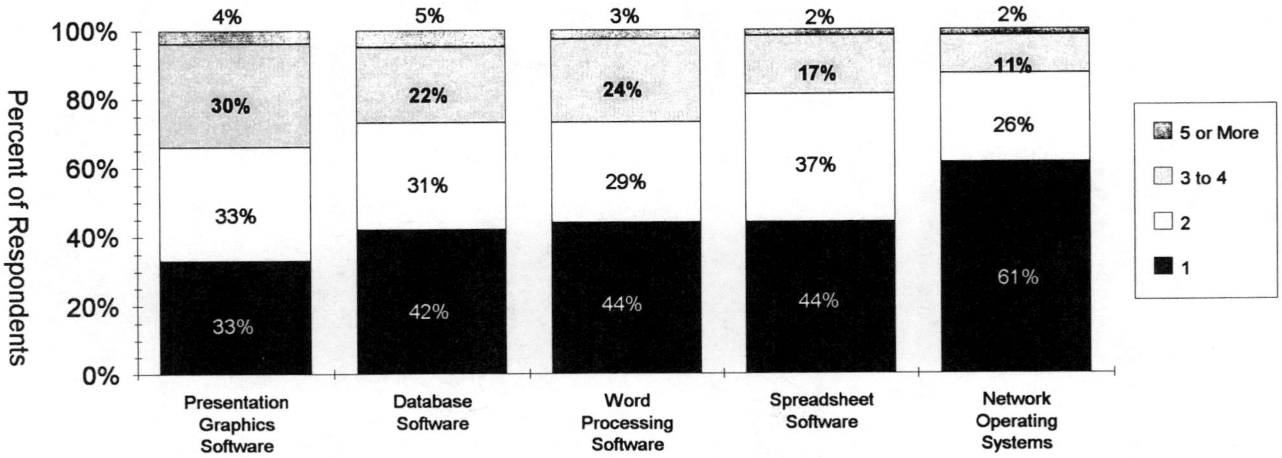

Legend:
- 5 or More
- 3 to 4
- 2
- 1

	Presentation Graphics Software	Database Software	Word Processing Software	Spreadsheet Software	Network Operating Systems
5 or More	4%	5%	3%	2%	2%
3 to 4	30%	22%	24%	17%	11%
2	33%	31%	29%	37%	26%
1	33%	42%	44%	44%	61%

Percent of Respondents (0% to 100%)

Source: International Data Group, "Buying I.T. in the '90s: How to Target," Boston, 1993, p. 42.

responses: articles and reviews in computer magazines and product advertising.[10] This data suggests that you should not let other parts of the marketing mix dilute your public relations and advertising program.

Once a product has been purchased, that product's position is strengthened considerably when the time comes for repurchase. This is because brand loyalty further tightens the already small consideration set for repeat purchases. IDG has found that across the range of computer products, from one-third to two-thirds of repurchasers are locked into the brand selected in the previous purchase. In its 1993 "Buying I.T. in the '90s" study, IDG asked business buyers to rate their likelihood of purchasing the same brand that they last purchased if they were to make a purchase decision today. Ratings on a nine-point scale (where 1 = not at all likely to repurchase and 9 = very likely to repurchase) were grouped into three clusters: switcher (1 to 3), fence sitter (4 to 8), and loyal (9). Against this high standard of brand loyalty, the results in Figure 1-3 are striking. This is an example of attitudes following behavior. If you can get a customer to buy your product once, she is much more likely to buy it again. For products with a high percentage of fence sitters, the opportunity to use brand marketing to build loyalty should be taken quickly before someone else beats you to it. It is still less expensive to keep fence sitters than to switch customers who haven't bought from you before.

Kelly Conlin, president of the IDG division responsible for the "Buying I.T. in the '90s" research, summarizes the stakes for computer product vendors in cultivating and maintaining a strong brand by saying, "If a vendor can build and sustain unaided awareness of its brand, its opportunity to generate first-time sales and lock in repeat purchases increases substantially. The power of branding in the information technology business is enormous, and our research suggests that it will only continue to grow."

Brand Equity

Brand equity can be defined as the added value provided to a product or company by its brand identity. It is the set of associations and behaviors that increase or decrease the value of the

Figure 1-3. Likelihood of repurchasing same brands as last purchase (business).

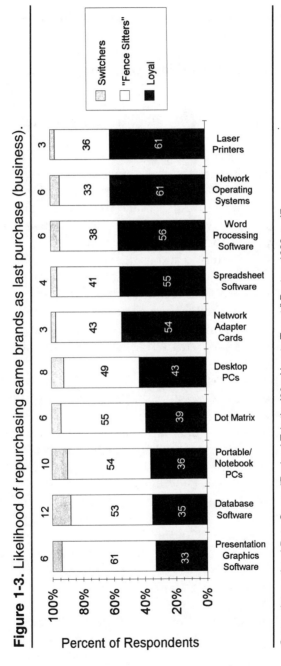

Source: International Data Group, "Buying I.T. in the '90s: How to Target," Boston, 1993, p. 47.

brand (company or product) compared to its financial value alone. Brand name awareness, proprietary brand assets (e.g., trademarks, patents, established channel relationships), brand associations, perceived quality, and brand loyalty are the categories for measuring the assets and liabilities that make up brand equity.[11]

"A brand has an equity quality to it. It's something you literally invest in," says Arthur W. Buerk, a partner in Shurgard Storage Systems and a Seattle-based businessman.

In 1977, he joined a company called BD Mini Storage. *B* and *D* were the first letters of the last names of the two founders, and Buerk convinced them that *B* and *D* weren't something they could build a strong equity around. "Since the name represented their own names, it was very difficult to get them to give it up," Buerk says, but eventually they changed the name to Shurgard—an excellent example of a brand name that is simple, easy to say, and unique, and that says quality and reliability. "After fifteen years," says Buerk, "it's become a brand and, in the storage industry, is probably considered the best brand name and has the best market position." Buerk explains that it was a matter of changing the company's positioning from being a real estate investment to becoming a national retail chain.

If you don't build a brand image around your company yourself, some kind of image will get built anyway, often by your competitors, and you can ultimately end up with an image that has little value. You can't let this happen. The difference between successful and unsuccessful people, according to Buerk, is that the successful people have a plan and the unsuccessful just let things happen. Building a brand is a conscious process. The difference between Coca-Cola and Charlie's Cola in terms of ingredients probably isn't much. Blindfolded, most people can't tell the difference in taste. But one has invested an incredible amount of money, integrity, and consistency in the process of building a brand. This has been done with great precision and integrity—from trucks to packaging to point of sale—and the company has ended up with an asset that's far greater than the product or the equipment.

"Brand equity is not just image; it's a strength, an inherent value, a leverage that a company can draw on as they introduce new products and that they can rely upon when the market gets tough," says Dave Roberts, worldwide advertising manager for

Claris Corporation. "When a category or an industry gets into a price war, customers will all of a sudden get interested in brand value, especially if it's just a 10 percent differential in price. Ten percent is not enough of a premium to take a risk."

For every impact, good or bad, that the brand has on customers, the company and product receive it back, with interest. In Eastern philosophy, this phenomenon is called karma. So, brand equity can be seen as business karma between companies, products, and customers. This is especially true with knowledgeable consumers. Therefore, brands don't belong entirely to the company; the customer is an essential and causative partner in the brand. Customers know that when they decide to buy or not buy a brand, and when they recommend or warn against a brand, they are rewarding or punishing not only the company, but the retailer or channel through which the product was distributed as well. One-way communication, from company to customer, is evolving to two-way communication, in which feedback from customers is a fundamental part of the company's marketing.

What has been proved over and over again is that companies that compete in crowded markets solely on the basis of price will fail. Can you think of one successful company that only touts price advantage? For a company to win when it is up against lots of competitors, customers have to think more than "lowest price"; they have to see lasting value. "Building brands is all about one thing: developing, defending, strengthening, and enduring profitable brand relationships," states Larry Light, chairman of the Coalition for Brand Equity. Strong brand identities have strong consumer franchises, generate customer pull (customers asking for the brand by name), and can be extended into new products.

When Rolls Royce was up for sale in 1973 to save itself from liquidation, offers came in from all over the world. However, when prospective purchasers discovered that only a British buyer would be allowed to keep the logo and "Spirit of Ecstasy" statuette, with their brand associations of "English class, quality and luxury, the Rolls Royce company was deemed to be worth neither dollar, yen nor mark."[12]

Brand name is king with mass merchants and retailers. According to Bob James, a PriceCostco buyer, the warehouse chain's premise "is to buy national brand products that are the leaders in their particular categories. In general, we only stock one SKU [i.e., specific product] in each category."[13] This alone should be enough motivation to be the number one brand in whatever category you're in.

The law of dominance says: One is wonderful, two is terrific, three is threatened, four is fatal. Marketers should aim to be number one or number two. The number three position is marginal, and fourth or worse is to be avoided at all costs.

Market leaders are more profitable. Furthermore, while to lead is good, to dominate is best. The PIMS study of 2,600 businesses showed that the greater the market share, the greater the return on investment. Products with a 40 percent market share get three times the return of products with only a 10 percent market share.[14] Of brands holding first, second, and third places in 1969, 91 percent were still alive twenty years later and 68 percent were in fourth place or better.[15] So, the objective is clear: Aim to dominate in every market in which you choose to compete.

Leading brands remain leaders. Eveready, Kodak, Gillette, Goodyear, Sherwin-Williams, and Singer have been leaders in their respective fields for decades. Think back to when you were young and the brands that your family used then. Aren't many of those brands still leaders? The reason that so many of the technology leaders of even the recent past are no longer leaders today is because they have neglected their brand.

If you're not tracking your brand and your competitors' brands, your competitors can be stealing market share without your catching on before it's too late.

Turning Fickle Customers Into
Your Company's Love Slaves

Some of the biggest players in the computer industry use brand building to maintain a competitive advantage. Hewlett-Packard, with its consistent message of high quality and reliability, and Intel, with its Intel Inside campaign, are two excellent examples of leaders that are intent on remaining leaders by not letting their brands become sullied by poor quality or become just another name in the pack. Microsoft consistently pounds home the messages of "safe buy" and "easy to use" in its advertising, and Apple Computer has become synonymous with "fun" for a whole generation of computer-savvy kids. Ask almost any schoolchild about his or her preference for a computer and you're likely to hear "Macintosh!" These leaders have managed to remain leaders because they understand the value of building loyalty to a company and its products.

Consider another example of a company that knows the value of brand. In May 1990, Symantec acquired the Peter Norton line of PC software utilities. Rod Turner, then Symantec's executive vice president in charge of the Peter Norton Group, said that at first he and others at the parent company did not understand how valuable the Peter Norton name was.[16] Research soon showed how much faith customers had in the Peter Norton name, and that they thought of Norton himself (usually featured prominently with arms crossed in ads for the software) as "the guy who saved their butts."

Needless to say, Symantec made the decision to maintain the Peter Norton name as a clear, viable brand. "If you do a good job over a long period of time and have a brand that's associated with that good job, then you have invested equity and are building an umbrella of credibility for new things that you do," says Turner. He goes on to say, "When we launch a new utility product, there is a predisposition on the part of the market to believe it is a better product because it comes from Norton. Of course, if we milk that and make a series of mediocre products, then we'll denigrate the brand over time and it will become useless to us. We continually reinvest in the brand to make it more and more powerful for us."

Trustmarket, Don't Demarket

A brand is much more than a trademark or a logo. It is a Trustmark, a promise of quality and authenticity. It identifies a company or product that customers can rely on, time after time. In the section "Brand Equity" we talked about the importance of rank and being a leader in your chosen market. Add reliability and reputation to rank, and you have the three Rs of brand building, as the purpose of a brand is to uniquely identify a company and its products, differentiating them from competitors. Brand enhances the perceived value, quality, and satisfaction a customer experiences. Brand provides a springboard for new products, helps build stable, long-term demand, and maximizes profitability.

High-tech *demarketers* focus on selling without adding value and building brand character. They look on ads as a cheap way to do a data sheet. They don't see the value in marketing—just in selling. They promote and offer price discounts to build volume rather than creating pull and consumer desire for the value in their brands. They don't spend a dollar on customer surveys. They see the job as being finished when the sale is made. They don't think brands need advertising support. They keep milking the cash cow after the poor cow has gone dry.

Trustmarketers build sales and brand value simultaneously. They advertise to reinforce the relationship current customers have with the brand and to attract new customers. They know that advertising builds customers' perceptions of quality. They work extra hard to keep their customers sold and loyal.

Here are two lists that show how a demarketing company can get caught in a descending spiral of reactions leading to failure and how a trustmarketing company can act to climb the ladder to success step by step.

The Descending Spiral of Demarketing

1. Situation: Urgent need for sales.
2. Reaction: Cut prices and shift marketing dollars from advertising into sales promotion.
3. Result: Increased volume, but lower margins.
4. Reaction: Reduce R&D spending, lower quality level, and cut advertising to maintain profitability.
5. Result: Loss of sales.
6. Situation: Urgent need for sales. . . .

The Ascending Ladder of Trustmarketing

1. Research customer needs and determine what builds their satisfaction and loyalty.
2. Advertise and publicize the brand.

3. See customer demand and volumes increase.
4. Raise price.
5. Get better margins.
6. Improve products.
7. Research customer needs and determine what builds their satisfaction and loyalty. . . .

To be a trustmarketer, build brands as assets, reject the view that the role of marketing communications stops at the sale, avoid undermarketing the market's leading brands, and measure loyalty, awareness, and consideration.

The most important factor, the foundation of every brand, whether a company brand or a product brand, is perceived quality. The extent to which customers believe that branded products are superior determines how high a price you can charge compared to generic competitors. The key is to focus on identifying customers' quality signals—that is, what they associate with quality. For example, with computers and software, speed is strongly associated with quality. There's one simple way to find out what your customers' quality signals are: Ask them in sufficient numbers that the results are projectable.

Branding Is for Customers, Too

Most companies view the role of brand advertising and marketing as attracting new customers. Of course, new customers are important. But a case can be made that the first priority is to retain customers. Why? Because it costs so much more to attract new customers.

Rather than solely focusing on the familiar "AIDA" (awareness, interest, desire, action) model, focus on moving current customers up the buyer tier, from occasional buyer to loyal customer to ally to advocate and evangelist. Software companies have discovered the easy bucks to be made by hiring a few people to generate hundreds of thousands, if not millions, of dollars by selling upgrades to their customer list through simply mailing a sales letter, flyer, and order form.

At Microsoft, approximately 30 percent of application software sales are to customers who are upgrading and 30 percent are to customers who are buying more Microsoft programs. Is it any wonder that with an 8.5-million-customer database and a 3-million-circulation newsletter, Microsoft is the industry's highest-circulation publisher?

Brands are about relationships between brand and buyer. In technology markets, advocates and evangelists ignite word of mouth. The romancing of enthusiastic computer users who influence between 40 and 50 percent of Microsoft's sales, although they represent less than 20 percent of the customer base, is a key marketing activity. The company spends over $100 million annually on customer service, such as customer help lines, to build customer satisfaction.[17]

Is Brand Building Worth the Trouble?

Brands give customers another whole set of reasons—both emotional and personal—to consider and buy, or switch. We are habitual in our use of brands, so brand switching advertising costs are usually high, requiring careful strategic planning. For example, people in transition are more likely to change brands; one change opens the door for other changes. Finding these people and reaching them at the right time with the right messages to get them to try the product is a good strategy in both business and consumer markets.

Branding is a good idea only if you want to strengthen customer loyalty, increase word-of-mouth recommendations, obtain a premium price and margins, and raise your company's worth. All of these results have been shown to stem from successful brand building.

So, how do you get people to perceive extra worth in your brands? First of all, perception is flawed. We all see the world through different glasses. Fortunately for marketers, a lot of people like wearing the same kind of glasses.

The trick is to find the commonalties in how people form perceptions and choose products. Build your brand identity around these perceptions. Schematically, the process looks like this: Perception Research → Brand Identity → Customer Choice → Brand Equity. Use human nature to your advantage. Most buyers are romanced or take sides or do what their peers do. But consumers are not dumb. Remember, they're your parents, spouse, and children.

Notes

1. "The Year of the Brand," *The Economist*, Dec. 24, 1988, 100.
2. Don Cowley, "Introduction," in *Understanding Brands*, ed. Don Cowley (London: Kogan Page Limited, 1991), 11.
3. Dawn Smith, "Compaq's Comeback," *Marketing Computers*, December 1993, 21–27.
4. Peter H. Farquhar, "Managing Brand Equity," *Journal of Advertising Research*, August/September 1990, RC-7.
5. Mary Lewis, "Brand Packaging," in *Understanding Brands*, ed. Don Cowley (London: Kogan Page Limited, 1991), p. 137.
6. The material in this section is copyrighted by Einstein 1993. Used by permission.
7. International Data Group, "Buying I.T. in the '90s: The Channels," Boston, 1992, p. 83.
8. International Data Group, "Buying I.T. in the '90s: The Channels," Boston, 1992, p. 87.
9. Research by IntelliQuest, Inc., cited in International Data Group, "Buying I.T. in the '90s: The Channels," Boston, 1992, p. 84.
10. International Data Group, "Buying I.T. in the '90s: The Channels," Boston, 1992, p. 96.
11. David A. Aaker, *Managing Brand Equity: Capitalizing on the Value of a Brand Name* (New York: The Free Press, 1991), 15–21.
12. "Corporate Clients Dismiss Design's Delusions," *Design & Art Direction*, Sept. 5, 1986.
13. Jeff Keller, "Born to Buy: A Day in the Life of a Buyer," *The Costco Connection*, November 1993, 10–11.
14. R. D. Buzzell and B. T. Gale, *The PIMS Principles: Linking Strategy to Performance* (London: Collier Macmillan, 1987).

15. David Mercer, "Death of the Product Life Cycle," *Admap*, September 1993, 15–19.

16. Rod Turner, "Brand Building in the Software Marketplace," Software Publishers Association Marketing Bootcamp, San Diego, Mar. 3, 1993.

17. Bradley Johnson, "In a Millisecond, Microsoft Boots Up Marketing Database," *Advertising Age*, Nov. 8, 1993, S6.

2

It's a Brand-New Market Out There

"The role brand plays is different now because the nature of the buying audience is changing dramatically."

C. E. "Charlie" Pankenier
IBM director of brand management

"There are many technology markets that are not involved in brand-based competition today, but will be in the near future."

Brian Sharples, president
IntelliQuest

- Computers and software now rub shoulders with VCRs and TVs on retailers' shelves.
- The PC industry is a much bigger market than TV and movies put together.
- Distribution channels change course like the Mississippi. What used to be the "normal" PC channel has widened to include superstores and supermarket retailing.
- The accelerating rate of technological change can reduce the term of one's competitive advantage to a few months.
- To top it off, the end user has become far more knowledgeable, confident, and even militant.

Still think it's the same old market out there? Then check out this fact: Of the top 100 U.S. business marketers ranked in 1993, 86 percent are technology companies. This is up from 75 percent in 1992 and 66 percent in 1991. More than $12 trillion in goods and services are sold in the United States each year, and business and government (not individual consumers) account for 64 percent of the spending.[1] Behind every consumer purchase are many sales transactions between firms.

That's why this book deals with TechnoBrands, not business brands. Historically, industrial or smokestack companies, such as DuPont (the company behind brand names such as Nylon and Chromalin), have been far better at brand building than upstart technology companies.

Technology markets have changed dramatically. Technology companies once targeted new users; now they target existing users looking for replacement products. Technology products once were unique; now their strength lies in being similar and compatible. What's more, there are more competitors, product benefits are short-lived, and prices have fallen. The end result: Buyers now differentiate on brand values that can be emotional as well as rational factors.

Interest in creating brands with high emotional content is growing fast, especially outside the packaged-goods area—in services, in business-to-business markets, and in technology. Businesspeople are realizing that the relationship customers have with a brand dramatically affects their view of the products that display the brand name and logo.

Are You Boiling to Death?

The gradual changes in high-tech marketing give the boiling-a-live-frog parable new meaning. If you drop a frog into boiling water, it will hop right out. But if you place the frog in a pot of cold water and gradually raise the temperature, it will just sit there and boil to death. Don't be like the frog. The brand issue is getting hot. Act while you are able.

How do smart executives get themselves into hot water unknowingly? We all have a tendency to get caught up in our daily problems and to choose to work on those projects we are comfortable with or enjoy. The result: In the race to push products out the door, manufacturers often emphasize features and performance and ignore the basic tenets of marketing—building a strong brand identity for themselves and for their products.

There are exceptions, of course. Hewlett-Packard Company, Intel Corporation, and Apple Computer come to mind. But our research reveals that generally, few high-technology companies or advertising agencies understand the value of going beyond the basic product sell by embedding brand values in their marketing communications materials, nor do they have a process in place to build brand equity.

This is not surprising. Most technology product manufacturers (and their advertising agencies) start from a position of product difference—a technological breakthrough of which they are justifiably proud. In contrast, in more mature consumer goods markets, new product developments are rarely groundbreaking; it's up to the agency to add the "differential" from a customer's perspective.

The problem is even worse when technology companies fail to understand that in highly competitive businesses—especially ones in which the products have become commodities—consistently growing market share over the long term isn't a matter of increasing performance, or decreasing prices, or running ads that swarm with black clouds of feature-laden copy. Rather, growing and maintaining market share comes from having customers who remain loyal to a product and a company because they make associations like "quality" and "reliability" when they see the brand. One of the most persuasive arguments for brand is customer retention; it costs four to six times as much to get a new customer as it does to retain one.

A Product Is Not Necessarily a Brand

Every successful brand embodies a product, but not every product is a brand. A product is something manufactured in a factory. A brand is something bought by the customer. The two are quite different. The brand is not tangible, something that engineers and technologists find uncomfortable. Brand represents the complete set of satisfactions the customer experiences. Products can be copied; trademarked brand names can't. Ironically, in the increasingly open marketplace of technology, brands are proprietary.

Go back ten years to the early days of the personal computer, when technology companies were technology companies and advertising agencies were advertising agencies (not the other way around, as some could claim today!). Few people need to be reminded who used Charlie Chaplin's friendly, approachable "Little Tramp" in its advertising. You may be surprised that it dates from 1983. The following year, who shook the world with its "1984" commercial? It was broadcast only once (during the third quarter of the Superbowl), but it liberated and empowered the individual. Besides virtually establishing the Macintosh personality overnight, the commercial, coordinated with public relations, sales promotion, and event marketing, was one of the first demonstrations of integrated marketing communications. Apple owes a lot to this commercial. Rather than talking about computers, it talked about how good computers make people's lives. Subsequent Apple advertising has continued to talk in the simplest and least technical terms possible.

A New Technology Marketing Paradigm

The early IBM and Apple advertisements both reflect the core values of the product, but that was ten years ago. So, what has happened since then?

To comment upon the changing market dynamics for technology products over the past ten years would require a book in its own right. The major changes can be summarized in the new technology paradigm shown in Figure 2-1. Although these changes are more evident in the United States, they also apply to Europe.

Technology companies have, by their very nature, always been engineering-led. Future success will be the territory of those that become marketing-led. The marketing paradigm in Figure 2-1 shows how the market has changed, but it gives little insight into the accelerating pace of change that should be anticipated in the future.

Figure 2-1. A New Technology Marketing Paradigm

Marketing Factor	Then	Now
Target audience	Professional	User
Purchase frequency	One at a time	Repeat
Channel	Dealer	Direct
R&D	Innovation	Joint venture
Differentiate by	Technology	Brand
Driving force	Engineering	Customer needs
Company orientation	Manufacturing/ engineering	Brand marketing
Public relations	Getting ink	Getting the right relationships
Communication	One way	Two-way dialogue
Consumer behavior	Social pressure	Rampant individualism
Quality	Styling, short life	Real quality, long life
Geographic scope	National	Local and segmented
Type communication	Verbal	Visual
Level of competition	Moderate	Aggressive
Production runs	Simple	Complex and customized
Number of media types	Few, TV dominant	Explosion in forms of media
Appeal	Features and benefits	Symbols, metaphors, and characters

The changes in the market are not over. The change is continual. I am encouraged that technology is becoming more people friendly, thus enabling the power of technology to make more people's lives richer and more productive.

How the IBM Brand Is Changing

One company grappling with the relationship of technology to people is IBM. "It's fair to say the IBM brand has been important to us, although the way the brand is important is changing," says C. E. "Charlie" Pankenier, IBM director of brand management.

Historically, the IBM brand and the sense of confidence it conveyed provided an entree that was hard for its competitors to duplicate or match. When gaining access to decision makers or when selling relatively new technologies, IBM had a tremendous advantage. Up until the late 1980s, many, if not most, competitors followed IBM developments intensely, looking for niches, or opportunities where they could get in and make sales without attracting IBM's attention. Not so today.

A brand is a promise in the consumer's mind of what you stand for. According to Pankenier, IBM stands for service, support, and a willingness to stand behind what it sells. IBM's willingness and ability to stand behind what it sells has added to the IBM brand equity over the years. Brand equity is more than words and pictures. It comes from what people accomplish in the customers' eyes; they have to be a real-life embodiment of the promise. "What we were selling wasn't just a product," Pankenier states. "It was a relationship and, in most cases, it was a fairly long-term and significant relationship, particularly for businesses where the information technology they were installing was fundamental to the successful operation of their business."

IBM's marketplace today is very different from its historical one. There are many more customer contact points and more diversity, not only in customers, but also in distribution channels and in the range of computer products and services provided. As a result, the customer relationship often operates at some distance from IBM people. Whether it's a PC bought through an electronics retailer or a business partner taking IBM's product, adding value of his or her own, and providing a solution for wholesale auto parts distribution, the IBM of today is largely removed from the actual transaction in the marketplace.

In this environment, living up to the brand promise becomes a different kind of proposition. In an increasingly competitive, crowded, and cluttered marketplace, the brand becomes more and more important as a way to have customers see their way through all the choices and alternatives in the marketplace and get to your offering.

The IBM brand, the Big Blue of tomorrow, can build on quality, technology, trust, service, and support. "We want to take all of those attributes from the past into the future," says Pankenier. "At the same time, there are a number of areas where we've got to do better, such as speed to market. The perception of IBM as nimble, responsive, or timely is important for us, not as a perception, but as a reality." For all companies, not just IBM, the promise ultimately has to be backed up by performance.

Short-Term Sales Pressure versus Long-Term Brand Equity Investment

What are the issues or problems that marketing communications managers in technology companies must deal with? First, the changing market has put pressure on them to gain short-term sales, at the expense of building long-term brand values. Take the case of four major computer advertisers in the United Kingdom whose ads stress price and specifications, with no brand building techniques used. They spent a total of £19.78 million on advertising in 1992 alone. Yet, not one of them can be considered a success story today. And this is merely the tip of a £170 million iceberg of United Kingdom advertising featuring technical specifications and prices.

Why is so much money being spent so unwisely? Many people assume that businesses, in particular, buy on price, but that is simply not the case. The findings of the IDG research discussed in Chapter 1 emphasize the importance of brand relative to price in corporate buyers' product decisions. Additional support for this point is found in other IDG research. Among the issues IDG has addressed is the content of corporate lists of approved products for department-level purchases. IDG found that brand is specified in these lists in 59 percent of surveyed companies, compared to the vendor being specified 40 percent of the time and features being specified 31 percent of the time.[2]

The conclusion to draw from this data: Resorting to price- and specification-based advertising is demarketing, which leads to lay-offs, losses, and unhappiness. To build stable, long-term demand and a healthy business, use TechnoBranding to help gain new customers (short-term sales) and to build the base of loyal customers who will *want* to buy from you whenever they have a need for your products.

It's also interesting to note that the emerging winners from the PC price wars have proved to be the strong brand-name vendors, not the no-name alternatives. As this is written, the large PC brands are killing off the no-name PC makers and, at the same time, seeing historic levels of demand.

That's not to say that strongly branded technology products can't compete on terms other than, or in addition to, price. Dell Computer Corporation, with its direct added service promise, is a classic example. You can order a PC direct from Dell with the software already loaded to your exact specifications. That's true value-added service from a manufacturer. The promise and the price are linked.

One of the ways in which Dell Computer stays competitive is by using research to deeply understand its customers. It studies "Techknowledge," people's relationship to technology, in America and Europe. Some of its more interesting findings include:

- The British are more "techno-tolerant" than fellow Europeans and Americans.
- Fully 46 percent of British, 50 percent of German, 55 percent of French, and 55 percent of Americans are "techno-phobic" (that is, fearful of and resistant to modern technology in their everyday lives).
- Yet, 76 percent of Americans believe that technology at home or at work makes their lives easier and enjoy the challenge of figuring out what technology can do.
- Among Americans, 85 percent agree that using computers

can save them time, and 80 percent feel that computers are fun to use.[3]

These last two points show why computer use in the home is rapidly rising, both for home business and for personal use. Companies that track these kinds of trends can be the first to exploit them.

As computer use grows, the market can be segmented in many ways to enable marketing to be personalized and made most relevant to buyer groups. Any kind of communication, whether an advertisement, brochure, or book, is easier to create if one has a definite picture in mind of the reader or recipient. For example, Dell has segmented its own customers into "Techno-Types":

- Techno-Wizards—Thrive in a high-tech environment: the hotter and more challenging the technology, the better.
- Techno-to-Go—May already have a good knowledge base, but want a computer that's ready to run right out of the box and prefer to call a customer assistance line for help than to refer to a manual.
- Techno-Boomers—May have started from ground zero, but studying hard to learn how computers can help them look smart.
- Techno-Novices—Want to look smart, yet have no knowledge of, or experience with, technology.
- Techno-Phobes—Avoid technology whenever possible. Pencil-and-paper types all the way!
- Techno-Teamers—Chief interest in computers is how computers can improve their productivity at the office and how computers can make them more valuable members of the corporate team.
- Techno-Critical—Rely on computers for more sophisticated applications critical to the job, such as computer-aided engineering or design.

Communicating and building a relationship with a Techno-Novice is much different from doing so with a Techno-Wizard. The more you can narrow your target market or audience, the better your branding messages and results will be.

Brand Premium = Profits

The economics of technology businesses is changing rapidly. A survey by McKinsey & Co. and IntelliQuest, Inc. quantified the premium price that corporate PC buyers will pay for various brands of PCs. At the time this research was conducted, IBM, Compaq, and Apple could command premium prices of $295, $232, and $195, respectively, on a particular configuration of PC. This premium was measured as the amount the average customer was willing to pay for identical product over a second-tier brand.

"Although brand-related price premiums have been substantially reduced in the PC industry due to increased competition, it is important to note that even small differences can have a tremendous impact on the bottom line," says Brian Sharples, president of IntelliQuest, Inc. "For example, Compaq's ability to charge a $232 premium on a PC with an average selling price of $2,500 adds 9.3 percent to the bottom line. In today's competitive markets, this can mean the difference between profit and loss at the corporate level."

One traditional way manufacturers have increased profitability is by cutting manufacturing, sales and marketing, and administration costs. In OEM (original equipment manufacturer) businesses, everybody buys the same components from the same companies and negotiates the same kinds of deals. When every company cuts head count and overhead, costs tend to approach parity. The one thing a company can do that is sustainable over time is build a brand-based competitive advantage.

"Developing a price advantage is the single biggest lever that a company can employ to boost margins and profits," says Sharples. In this paradigm, the focus shifts from minimizing product costs to maximizing the premium price that can be charged. Cost advantage used to be a powerful weapon, but in most mature technology markets, significant cost advantages are becoming harder to develop. What do you do when all of the major players in your markets have made similar cuts in their corporate costs and you find the potential new margin erased by further rounds of price cutting? Sustainable margin advantage is no longer a function just of cost, but of the price premiums gained through brand strength.

How quickly is the idea of branding taking off with technology companies? "It is, without a doubt, one of the most discussed topics in our industry, and the measurement of brand strength has become a significant part of our high technology research practice," Sharples says. "Technology executives in mature markets have fully embraced the concept of branding, although companies in new and emerging markets tend to focus more on technology-based competition."

Why is this? Most technology markets have a predictable life cycle. New markets often start with a single company that has a new idea or technology that solves a specific, unmet market need. This company's success attracts other companies that compete to meet that same market need, but with different approaches and products. In this stage of the product life cycle, the basis of competition is features and technology, not brand. Customers evaluate solutions on their technical merit.

As markets mature, creative technology solutions give way to standards as the market begins to define and demand a compatible and standardized approach. In this phase, more companies are attracted to the market opportunity, and the basis of competition begins to move beyond product features to service, support, and long-term company stability—all characteristics of a company brand.

"There are many technology markets that are not involved in brand-based competition today, but will be in the near future," Sharples predicts. It all depends on where your company and its products are in the market's life cycle. Forward-thinking executives start building brand strength early, because they understand the likely payoff from this investment down the road. "Unfortunately, many executives believe that they compete in markets where the products are too technically complex to ever be selected on the basis of brand strength," says Sharples. "Time has shown that what seems unique and complex to a buyer today will eventually become a more standardized purchase."

The earlier you start building brand, the easier it will be, and the less it will cost. When you look at how straightforward building brand really is, and that it doesn't conflict with anything during the early technically based market phase, TechnoBranding makes a lot of sense. Take Hewlett-Packard in the laser printer market today. IntelliQuest tracks customer awareness for laser printers, as well as other technology products. According to Sharples, "The brand lead they [HP] have built is so strong that it is virtually impossible for other printer companies to catch up without spending massive amounts of resources and money on advertising and other awareness and image-generating activities."

While some companies are only starting to think about brands, others are constructing elaborate brand strategies. For example, Compaq has different brands targeted at different customers: the Presario line of home computers and the ProLinea line of entry-level business computers. Dell offers its line of OptiPlex MX and NexPlex low-cost, high-performance PCs. AST has a value line of Bravo notebook and desktop PCs. Indeed, nearly every major PC manufacturer strives to improve brand strategy. Next will be different "flavors" of computers for different sales channels, such as warehouse clubs and superstores. Certainly, one basic box no longer works; look for more individualized brands, targeted at carefully researched market segments.

Changes in Our Society

What's happening in our society and how does it affect your business? We've moved from feeling comfortable and secure to feeling anxious and at risk. Because of the accompanying stress, we're looking for anything familiar, pleasurable, and satisfying to balance our fear of the future and to give us a sense of control over our lives. This kind of emotional change provides an ideal environment for brands with value. Make customers feel secure, in control, and good about their selection of your brands, and they will be strongly predisposed to come back for more of the same.

Customers want open and candid communication. They look for actions, not words. For example, when buying a can of tuna fish, some people are just as concerned with how it was caught as they are with how it tastes. And the tuna companies have responded to those concerns, stating on the can that the product is "dolphin-safe." This shows that we live in a customer-driven marketplace. Software companies also listen to their customers and bring out new releases with hundreds of fixes and improvements.

We can see the importance of branding everywhere. Even the Catholic church is branding. For the Pope's visit to Denver in August 1993, the church authorized the first merchandising campaign for "Pope products," including everything from the standard T-shirts to the Pope-Scope, a periscope that enabled viewers to see the Pope over the heads of the people in front of them.

Kids, in particular, are fanatically brand loyal. According to a report entitled "Things Are Falling Apart: Portrait of a Generation," by Collett Dickenson Pearce, the "twenty something" generation, Generation X, places more faith in brands than in the police or the church.[4]

What does this mean for technology products? The good old days of high-tech marketing are over. Technology differences have been replaced by standards and sameness. Distribution channels are broadening and expanding.

In our complex and confusing world, brand is needed as an "editor." Brands symbolize the safe choice; they simplify decisions, eliminate surprises, and guarantee quality. Private-label brands become popular in recessions and when people are uneasy, watching dollars, and becoming value-conscious. Private-label brands are forcing cuts in corporate overhead, bloated by years of big profits. The pricing pressure is forcing companies to bring in better information systems to manage inventories and cost structures. And it's also getting managers away from volatile pricing schemes based on promotions that devalue the brand and the products themselves.

Computer advertising is beginning to return to real "brand value" advertising. For example, in September 1993, IBM ads in Europe featured designs developed in consultation with environmental protection groups, emphasizing lower power usage ("help save the earth"), recyclability, and "finally, ecology meets technology."[5]

The Demise of Product Life Cycles, Enter Brand Life Cycles

Products and their features come and go, brands remain. The traditional view of product life cycles (introduction, growth, maturity, and decline) pales in financial significance in comparison to the long-term stability of brand names. Product life is determined by market actions, but it should not be the point around which companies base their marketing programs. The brand life cycle is significantly longer than the planning horizons—and indeed, longer than the management tenure—of most companies. Japanese high-tech companies religiously develop 100+-year plans.

The use of the product life cycle model may even be dangerous because it leads to a belief that the product will mature and die, whereas the research on brands proves that strong brands live on and on.

What it ultimately comes down to is not markets, but individuals' attitudes toward brands, how people relate to brands, and how the brand adapts itself to the individual's psychology.

The switch to a customer-based brand orientation from a product orientation marks a significant trend in high-tech. IBM, HP, and others are switching to a brand management organization structure in which everything centers on the customer. Shouldn't you?

Notes

1. Jan Jaben, "Marketing's New Fast Lane Emerges," *Business Marketing*, October 1993, 20–21.
2. International Data Group, "Buying I.T. in the '90s: The People, The Patterns, and The Purchase," Boston, 1992, 91.
3. Dell Computer Corporation, "1993 Techknowledge in Europe and America," press materials dated Sept. 20, 1993, Bracknell, Berkshire, U.K.
4. Alex Benady, "Faith in Brands Tops Faith in Authority," *Marketing*, Aug. 19, 1993.
5. IBM, "It Isn't the Office of the Future. It's the Computer of Today" advertisement appearing in the *Economist*, Sept. 11, 1993; IBM, "The Future Has Arrived a Little Sooner than Expected," advertisement appearing in the *Harvard Business Review* (U.K.), September/October 1993.

3

Consumer Branding Is One Thing, Techno-Branding Is Another

"It's very hard for technology companies to embrace branding because technology and branding are complete opposites. To me, branding is consistency, consistency, consistency and technology is change, change, change. They clash."

Derrith Lambka, corporate advertising manager
Hewlett-Packard Company

"In entertainment software, the title is the brand. The company is like the Good Housekeeping seal. It doesn't draw people in; it closes the sale."

Mike Isaacson, director of corporate marketing
Sierra On-Line, Inc.

Can you tell the difference between consumer branding and technology branding? There's a tendency to say they're one and the same. That type of thinking can prove fatal to your brand-building efforts.

Just for fun, assign a "C" for consumer-based products or a "T" for technology-based products to each of the following eight characteristics. *Hint*: You have four of each.

____ simple	____ shorter life cycle
____ business use	____ impulse purchase
____ complex	____ personal use
____ longer life cycle	____ considered purchase

You'll learn the answers in a moment. The important thing to recognize is that there are differences. Too often, practitioners of traditional consumer branding, advertising, and marketing don't make the distinction.

That's because TechnoBranding is a new concept in marketing for high-technology companies. TechnoBranding is a systematic process for building technology brands. It takes the best from consumer branding and applies it to the different set of market conditions that technology companies face.

Now, let's see how they differ and how you did.

Consumer products are often simple commodities; technology-based products are complex. Consumer products are typically for personal use; technology products are most often for business use. Consumer products tend to have longer life cycles; technology products have shorter life cycles. Purchases of consumer products are often impulse decisions; technology products are generally considered purchases. This means that consumer marketers hired by technology companies and advertising agencies with a packaged-goods branding orientation need to be very careful about how they apply their consumer branding knowledge to technology marketing problems.

Buying a technology product is different from picking a bar of soap or a box of raisins off a store shelf. Technology purchasers possess a much higher degree of interest in and sophistication about the products they intend to buy, and at some point in the purchase process—probably sooner rather than later—they'll want more detailed information. They often buy on behalf of companies and are spending big chunks of money, so they will be demanding. They will also look closely at issues such as hardware and software compatibility and post-purchase support provided by the manufacturer.

Marketing technology products is different from marketing consumer products for two reasons:

1. The *customers* are different. You target the market for a technical product by job function, not by demographic profile. Also, more people get involved in the approval of technology-based products, and buyers face limits on purchase authority.
2. The *channels* are different. In selling technology, the sales and distribution channels typically play a larger and strategic role in the success of the product. Plus, the makeup of the channels is shifting and evolving rapidly.

These differences don't mean that we throw out consumer brand marketing—just the opposite. They mean that we use consumer brand marketing, but adapted in a special way to technology products, markets, and buyers.

What TechnoBranding Takes from Consumer Branding

The brand marketing concepts created a hundred years ago to sell Ivory soap provide a tremendous wealth of knowledge and experience that can be put to use selling high-tech products today. For starters, the definitions of branding terms like brand equity and brand associations are the same. Techniques for identifying brand associations and evaluating brand extension strategies translate directly. The technology industry has a lot to learn from consumer branding in gaining the discipline to work on annual and longer-term plans and adequately funding marketing communications to make sure the measured objectives are met. The most important thing to learn from consumer branding is the unrelenting focus on the customer's perspective of the brand.

"It makes no difference whether it's a high-tech company or a consumer-tech company, or a consumer product; when you're talking about branding, you're talking about developing an image and a relationship with your customer," says Jerry Gibbons, currently senior vice president of the western region for the American Association of Advertising Agencies (A.A.A.A.). "You do it by knowing who you are and knowing who your customer segments are, and speaking to those segments in terms that are relevant to them. What is important is that companies know what they are, know what they stand for—both for themselves and for their product—and that they really, truly understand their consumers."

Emotion Sells

Emotion is the most powerful tool in the technology brand marketer's toolkit. When you talk about image and relationship, emotion is at the center of everything you do. The better you can understand the emotional basis for your customers' relationship with your brands, the better you can appeal to it and use it to strengthen your customer bonds. In general, TechnoAds should be emotionally based and based on human rather than technical factors.

My favorite way of demonstrating the effect of emotion is to show people the Calvin Klein Escape perfume advertisement. Emotion is hard to understand intellectually, but easy to grasp. In one nationwide study, 22,000 consumers were asked about print advertising campaigns they'd seen and which one they ranked outstanding. Calvin Klein was ranked first in 1991 and second in 1992 (after Nike).[1] Once you've seen the Calvin Klein advertisement for Escape perfume, it's hard to forget it. This ad doesn't need a lot of copy to get the point across. It has the word "ESCAPE" at the top of the page, "Calvin Klein PERFUME" at the bottom, and in between, a man and a woman in an erotic position on a beach. Here are one woman's comments on the ad:

> This is a good ad. The black and white makes it so. This allows my imagination great projective play—that could be my beach, my swimming suit, my stones. The textures of sand and one-third page of stones is good. And the choice of white bathing suits give an odd contrast of purity or innocence to a familiar "hot" scene. Besides, the perfume is wonderful. I saw the ad, smelled the perfume, and went out and bought it. This is the only perfume I've ever bought for myself.

This ad is powerful. It gets right past all the barriers we set up to filter out all the messages that bombard us daily. It isn't intellectual. It isn't rational. It speaks to women's hearts and emotions.

In Europe, a similar situation exists with Häagen-Dazs' print ads, which show naked or seminaked couples in erotic poses eating ice cream. It is a controversial and often criticized campaign, but it is also one of the most successful product launches of recent times, as recognized by its winning an Institute of Practitioners in Advertising "Advertising Effectiveness Award," one of the most sought-after awards because to win it, a company needs to prove the effect of advertising on sales.

My point is not that you should use sex or emotion for their own sake. Rather, based on a profound understanding of your customers' psyche, you should relate to and explicitly recognize the emotional ties between customer and brand in your branding program.

Why is it that good advertising and marketing are accepted as natural and essential when selling cosmetics or groceries to women, but seldom when selling expensive products to men?[2] Many high-tech executives still believe that brand is only the province of the supermarket. In fact, it should be acknowledged that the consumer purchases referred to so cavalierly are actually bought by purchasing experts, individuals who shop every week, try out different products and different retailers, and learn from their experiences. The so-called big-ticket business purchase is often a one-time purchase that does not get the benefit of this experimentation and learning. This makes branding strategy even more important because buyers are afraid of making the wrong purchase decision. Fear is a very powerful emotion. By creating an aura of reliability, safety, and quality around your brands, you make them magnets of security for the cautious and conservative buyer.

Why is it that women office computer users outnumber men by more than two to one, but computer companies are still selling to men?[3] Why hasn't a computer company figured out how to relate to women computer users? Simple. No one has done the in-depth research and testing needed to understand the behavioral and emotional dynamics associated with marketing to women in a

Figure 3-1. Differences between consumer and technology products.

Consumer Brand Building	Technology Brand Building
Products for personal and family use	Products for business use
Simple products	Complex business products
Need to magnify a small feature into a differentiator or unique selling proposition: Ivory soap—"It Floats"	Need to distill an array of features into a single idea: Microsoft—"Making It Easier"
Quick consumption	Ongoing long-term relationship
No training needed	Training-dependent
Impulse decision	Considered purchase
Reach for a package on the shelf	Study spec sheets, request capital, obtain purchase approvals

technological context. Yes, it's subtle, and filled with cultural land mines, but the opportunity is huge.

Differences between Consumer And Technology Brand-Building

The accompanying charts clarifying the differences between consumer and technology brand building will help you apply this knowledge to your own marketing.

The Products

Figure 3-1 shows the differences between consumer and technology products.

The basic difference between consumer and technology product marketing is technology's accent on features. Branding is more important for technology products than for consumer products because it's more difficult to generate an emotional response from technology customers.

According to Norm Levy, a business strategist who heads Strategic Development Corporation, "The more technological and complex the product is, the greater the need for specific brand identity that the consumer can relate to with an emotion that's predictable."

Brand identity goes beyond just product marketing. Levy defines brand equity in its broadest sense as "the sum total of the confidence of all the stakeholders and their confidence in their company to achieve its intended future position." Stakeholders include not only customers but investors, suppliers, employees, and the general community. Strategically, brand should not focus exclusively on the customer, but should also focus on investors' and employees' perspectives of the brand.

"Brand equity is a foundation concept that can be applied universally to all stakeholders' perspectives. The key," Levy says, "is to move the perception of each stakeholder to a higher notch, which thereby increases the strategic equity of the company."

The Markets

Now let's look at the differences between consumer and technology markets, as shown in Figure 3-2.

Change is a given in all markets, but it is extremely rapid in technology markets. And technology markets can be very complex. This is particularly evident in the channels of distribution for the computer industry. Channels of distribution refers to the choices a company makes concerning how its products get sold to the final customer. Does a company sell direct to the customer, or should it use distributors and dealers (retail stores)? Or should it sell to various types of middlemen, systems integrators, and value-added resellers (VARs), who sell its product as part of a total solution?

These are critical questions not only for new companies but for existing companies. For example, if a company fails to recognize that its customers would prefer to buy from a middleman, who acts as both a purchase consultant and an ongoing provider

Figure 3-2. Differences between consumer and technology markets.

Consumer Brand Building	Technology Brand Building
Evolutionary	Revolutionary
Gradual change	Changes are often sudden and sweeping
New and improved	Completely new product categories
Purchase authority usually not an issue	Buyer often has limits on purchase authority
I see it. I want it. I buy it.	Multiple influencers
Audience targeted by demographics	Audience targeted by job function
Longer product life cycles	Short product life cycles
Basic product attributes remain unchanged, with evolutionary upgrades in packaging or functionality	New versions or complete product makeovers are expected; the upgrade path counts
Channels of distribution are stable	Channels are fluid and changing

of personalized service and support, than from the company's traditional outlets, it could quickly lose market share. If you have a gut feeling that your channels of distribution need to be looked at, act quickly to understand the dynamics at work and make appropriate and timely changes.

TechnoBranding in the Channel

The complexities of technology brand-building marketing are particularly evident in the branding issues associated with channels of distribution. Should your brand be developed only to reach the final end user, or should you focus on the marketing, sales, and distribution channels? The answer depends on whether your product falls at the "highly technical" or the "mass market" end of the spectrum. Let's hear what a leading consultant in this area has to say about this issue.

"There's a major battle going on between the forces in the industry that favor branding as the principal means of convincing a final customer to select a particular manufacturer's product versus the forces that advocate putting the choice of manufacturer and a particular product in the hands of the channel," observes Peter Raulerson of ParaTechnology, Inc., a Bellevue, Washington–based research and consulting firm.

As many as 30,000 companies in the United States are channel members in the computer industry. Channel members are those organizations and individuals that buy, resell, and influence the purchase of other companies' products. The term *channel* includes distributors, dealers, agents, consultants, and others (e.g., systems integrators and VARs) who don't simply stock and resell products, but also influence their selection. Perhaps half of all computer industry product sales either flow through or are directly influenced by channel members who decide, and then recommend to the final customer, which brand to buy.

Branding a product is as important for the channel members as for the final end user. Clearly, channel members are interested in what's important to the end user. The channel members are also interested in other things, like how they're going to make money.

"There's no doubt that when a new kind of technology gets introduced, it needs to be adopted by not only the influential customers but by influential channel members who 'make a market' in new technologies," states Raulerson.

For new or complex technologies that haven't reached mass market or commodity status, you need to make sure your marketing communications reach not only the final buyers and customers, but all the intermediaries, or channels, as well.

Most intermediaries for products at the mass market end of the spectrum are more interested in the business relationship they're going to have with a product's manufacturer than in the product itself. Many of the dealers, distributors, wholesalers, mass merchants—the people who sell computer hardware and software in volume—don't care what the product is or does. Executives of those firms are retailers or inventory specialists, and as long as the inventory turns are high and the margin is acceptable, it could just as well be soap or chicken as an electronics product. Raulerson says that branding there has to be full of images such as "this product's in demand," "this supplier is reliable," and "we know how to keep buyers coming back for more!"

The opposite is true at the other end of the spectrum, where we're talking about other channel members like systems integrators or VARs or computer consultants. They need to hear, "this product is viable," "you can build your business around it and not get burned," "the supplier offers you (the reseller) profitability you can plan on," and "you can make money by adding value to our product, and we will show you how to do this."

It's natural for manufacturers to want to leap from a new technical idea and a new technology to mass-market distribution as quickly as possible. To achieve that leap, to the extent that they think about positioning and branding at all, they look for characteristics—or claim characteristics for their product—that fit high-volume, mass-market distribution.

"That's detrimental to getting the product into the market and to achieving its initial success and building momentum," according to Raulerson. "In that area, more typically for a new type of technology or a new approach to a technical problem, you'd be looking more for messages that relate to low-volume, selective distribution through integrators and VARs."

The companies that have had the greatest success with complicated products, like local area networks, or products that require the user to have technical expertise, like database software, have found a particular niche (Macintosh) or created a differentiating benefit (works on many platforms) that separates them from their competitors and have maximized that—just pushed it as hard and fast as they could.

Some techniques for developing consumer brands are the inverse of what works for these technical brands. For example, in consumer brands, you want to know what thousands of people will think of, or how thousands of people will respond to, a given position or image, and so you look for a low common denominator. With complex technical products, however, you want to know what the opinion leaders are going to identify with. Then, you

Figure 3-3. Differences between consumer and technology brand values.

Consumer Brand Building	Technology Brand Building
Tend to be constant over time	May have to take into account values that change as the market evolves
Quality of life	Performance
Lifestyle benefits important	Audience looking for competitive edge
Familiarity and reliability important	Return on investment, ongoing costs, and price/performance important
I can count on this product	I need to make sure that this purchase decision is the right one and won't cost me my job
Self-image	Image at work
Largely built on emotional values	Usually incorporates rational values as well

want these opinion leaders to mention and recommend the product in their research reports, columns, or conversations.

Raulerson cites a number of examples: SynOptics, the leader in the network hub market; Oracle, the leader in database software; and Novell, the leader in network software. "They all created a fan club among the technical innovators, and that fan club extolled the virtues of the product. Besides constituting the early adopter segment, they acted as missionaries to the rest of the market."

Brand Values

We've looked at the product and market differences between consumer and technology marketing. Now, in Figure 3-3, let's look at some of the differences in values, those intangible human-based aspects of brand building that are deemed desirable and important by customers and market influencers.

Consumer brand building is typically built around the consumer's lifestyle and self-image using emotional values. This becomes quickly evident when watching commercials on prime-time TV shows. In technology brand building, there are two overriding brand values that must be taken into account: fear and performance. Brand identity can make buyers feel good about their purchase and relieve any doubts or fears they may have about making the right purchase decision. But brand identity will not cover up for a deficient product with inadequate performance and does not take the place of an effective sales force.

The Way It's Always Been Done Is Probably Wrong

Technology brand builders need to be quick on their feet! What was true last year is not necessarily true this year. The way it's always been done is probably the wrong way now. That's why the most successful leaders in the industry, people like Bill Gates and John Sculley, are so intensely and fully involved in their businesses. Most technology businesses are not amenable to absentee ownership.

How do all the differences between consumer and technology brand building figure into brand planning and strategy? If you come from a consumer background where campaigns are measured in years and product changes are infrequent, you could spend too much time creating the campaign. By the time you're finally done, the market could be heading in a totally different direction.

The point is, don't make too many assumptions about technology brand building based on packaged-goods experience. Do research the customers carefully. Do understand which messages they respond to and which ones they don't. In some technology markets, turning features into benefits can be insulting to customers. For example, many electronics engineers become disgusted by ads that list benefits for features. They want the facts and specifications and are smart enough (usually very smart) to understand what the features mean to them. In contrast, a woman buying perfume doesn't need to be told the list of extracts and ingredients and the dimensions of the bottle, or to be presented with a list of features and benefits that justify the perfume's appeal and explain its function. This is one key reason why research is important. You don't want your current and prospective customers to feel that they're being talked down to, or to feel that you are insulting them. The advantage of emphasizing emotional attributes and brand values is that they transcend specific features and benefits, which go out of date very quickly.

Just as computer and telecommunications technologies are converging, the differences between consumer products and technology products are growing smaller. I'm sure you thought of exceptions as you read the tables above. Entertainment, games, and educational software can be viewed as consumer products or simply toys. PCs themselves are a mass-market phenomenon.

A strong case can be made that technology/industrial marketing and consumer marketing are more similar than different.[4] One could argue that distinctions between TechnoBranding and consumer branding establish artificial boundaries that inhibit marketing advancement and stifle creativity. As a matter of fact, one could say that the differences *within* technology marketing and consumer marketing are greater than those that distinguish the two areas.

The fact is, there are no easy answers. The purpose of listing differences is not to arrive at *the* answer. The purpose is to inspire questions and to start you thinking outside the limits of conventional thinking. The boundary between technology/industrial buying and consumer buying is blurred and curved. In both consumer and technology markets, successful branding means some combination of customer research, brand definition and product differentiation, excellence in creativity, and, often, just being in the right place at the right time (luck).

Crossing the TechnoChasm

How can technology companies "cross the chasm" into consumer markets? In late 1993, Microsoft rolled out its well-financed Microsoft Home line of consumer software with $150 to $200 million in up-front money. That's more than the total annual revenues of all but a handful of software companies.[5] Bill Gates claims that Microsoft Home will be the biggest part of the company in five years. How will a company so tightly associated with business make the transition to consumer products? On the one hand, the Microsoft brand name is well known (it has a 99 percent recognition rating, according to Techtel Corp.), and the company has invested in over 450 employees to create and generate excitement among consumers for 100 multimedia, education, and fun-oriented titles. On the other hand, selling software to home-based consumers is a lot different from selling Excel spreadsheet software to businesses.

The transition will require a careful extension and delicate leveraging of the Microsoft brand name. From business values to values of fun, status, cool, and emotion. From complex, problem-solving software to software that is easy to use and fun.

Microsoft has proved to be capable of handling challenges like these with great success. If the Pillsbury Doughboy and the Jolly Green Giant can imbue sticky bland stuff and green vegetable balls with personality, character, and, most importantly, memorability, think what technomarketers like those at Microsoft can do with feature-rich products that possess tremendous depth and richness.

Who's Best? Consumer or High-Tech Ad Agencies?

Both consumer and high-tech ad agencies have a lot to learn about branding high-tech products and companies. Specialist, high-tech agencies need to develop their branding capabilities. Traditional agencies have a lot to learn about technology and how technology buyers think. Creative teams need to be passionate about sputter disk technology, for example, if they are to inspire the customer. If the creative team's aspiration is to work on the agency's big consumer account and they see the high-tech client only as a stepping-stone to bigger and better things, you certainly aren't going to get their best work.

All agencies must understand that *why* something is being bought is often more important than *what* is being bought. Whoever does so fastest will stand to gain the most.

How do you find the best agency to build your TechnoBrand?

Here are a few questions to ask during the agency review process:

- How important do you think brand building is for our products, and why?
- What is your process for building brands?
- Who will be doing the day-to-day work on our account, and what relevant brand-building experience do they bring to us? (Demand that only the people who will be active on your account be in the presentation.)

Now, let's look at branding in more detail.

Notes

1. Kevin Goldman, "Risk Paid Off in 1992 Print Campaigns," *Wall Street Journal*, May 18, 1993, p. B6.
2. William Rees-Mogg (editor of The [London] *Times*), Advertising Association Conference, 1980; quoted in Jeremy Bullmore, *Behind the Scenes in Advertising* (Henley-on-Thames, Oxfordshire: NTC Publications Ltd.), 1991, 125.
3. Rachel Kaplan, "The Gender Gap at the PC Keyboard," *American Demographics*, January 1994, 18.
4. Edward F. Fern and James R. Brown, "The Industrial/Consumer Marketing Dichotomy: A Case of Insufficient Justification," *Journal of Marketing*, Spring 1984, 68–77.
5. Sharon M. Baker, "For a Home Run, Microsoft Needs to Pitch to Consumers," *Puget Sound Business Journal*, 14, no. 21 (1993); 1 and 48.

4

The TechnoBranding
Process

"Make brand management as important as R&D in your organization, because TechnoBranding is the most powerful innovation since the microprocessor."

Neil Stewart and Chuck Pettis speaking to the
World Industrial Advertising Congress

"The Road to Hell is paved with companies who developed their technology, but neglected their brand."

Floathe Johnson

How do you build a TechnoBrand? First, the basics must be in place. That means you need a quality product that meets a real-world need, and you need a well-run business. Starting with that base, the process of TechnoBranding begins.

We have already talked in general about TechnoBranding. Now, let's get specific. TechnoBranding is:

- A strategic approach and philosophy of communications based on the premise that building a technology brand is different from building a consumer brand
- A systematic process for creating a technology company's brand
- A "technology" that can be used to research, define, create, and manage brands of all kinds

TechnoBrands are especially important now in technology markets because of the increased number of competitors and powerful brands extending their reach to cash in on profitable market niches as they begin to emerge. Managers in corporations can't afford to make a mistake with a big, expensive, visible purchase. In coping with downsizing, the threat of layoffs, and budget tightening, managers look for the safe buy, and they need reinforcement that they made the right decision.

The Changing Role of Branding in High-Tech

In the early days of the high-tech industry, only two types of people were comfortable making a buying decision: those who were confident of their technical knowledge and a relatively low number of "visionaries willing to take a risk," as consultant and author Geoffrey Moore describes them.

Because most people spent so much time analyzing the choices, branding wasn't seen as a critical factor; any mystique a brand might create was stripped away during the analysis process.

However, now that the industry is in its second and third generations, people in the marketplace have grown more familiar with products. As prices have come down and more products have become standards, such as the HP LaserJet 4 and Microsoft DOS 6.0, people have gained confidence in their ability to make a choice. At this point, having a strong brand identity is critical. Getting that brand identity, though, is a function of lots of planning and work early on in the market's evolution.

Moore sees brands as, first, an expression of a company's history in the marketplace and, second, a desire to have the purchase meet psychographic needs, not just utilitarian needs. He believes that this is particularly true with discretionary items like screen savers, pop-up utilities, mouse pads, mice, carrying cases, and other accessories.

"TechnoBranding as a subdiscipline of branding is correct," Moore believes. "It's a piece of the puzzle, like having a secret ingredient, that has been used in consumer packaged goods, and [is illustrated by] 'Intel Inside' and 'Postscript from Adobe.'" However, that's not to say that there won't still be some anxiety or worry about making the right purchase. Therefore, a brand strategy that just says "trust my brand" won't work.

Brand and brand building are common in many consumer-products companies, but technology companies have not, to a large extent, embraced brand building. Why is this? Have consumer-product marketers kept brand building a secret? Or does it have more to do with the nature of a youthful industry pioneered not by marketers but by engineers, and a lack of good role models?

Consumers, even business-to-business consumers, see brand as a promise. The promise is different for every brand. For a Microsoft product, the consumer knows that the promise is compatibility and "making it easy." For a Borland product, the promise is value. For a Sierra On-Line game, the promise is play value. For Traveling Software's LapLink, the promise is file transfer done well. And so on.

Helen Manich, executive director for cellular marketing with US West NewVector Group, points out that 100 years ago, names of businesses stood for something real instead of being simply an element of advertising as they are today. Usually the company was named for the owner(s)—for example, Sears and Roebuck really were the founders of the business.

Similarly, Manich believes that brands for high-tech services need to be friendly and personable because high-tech can intimidate people and make them feel stupid, which is not an enjoyable feeling. "Marketing is about having some fun; if names aren't fun, they don't invite people in," Manich says.

People also need to know immediately what's in it for them; by telling them the benefits, you invite them in and begin a relationship. You then need to say, "If this isn't right for you, I'll get out of the way; but if it is right, I want to help." In order to intrigue people, though, it's got to be fun.

Manich was at MCI when the company started the "Friends and Family" campaign. The title of the campaign was based on the fact that friends and family are who you call from home; the strategy was to reach the heart. Because people tend to make decisions with their hearts and then justify their decisions with their minds, first impressions are everything in advertising.

The first ten seconds will either turn people on or turn them off. If you are elitist and exclude people in your marketing approach, they'll exclude your product from their decision set. You've got to romance both parts—the intellect and the heart—or people won't feel comfortable that your product mirrors their lives. To be successful, you need to deliver products and services in a way that supports the brand, that supports romance.

"The last time I talked with a customer service representative at MCI about my service," Manich recounts, "he concluded the call by asking, 'Helen, have I done everything I possibly can to satisfy your telephone needs?' I've never been asked that question by another company. I hung up and said, 'Wow, we've got to start asking that question!' "

That kind of one-on-one warmth and power reinforces the brand name, the "friends and family" promise. So it's important to ask yourself, "Does our behavior reinforce the image we want?"

"As a marketer," Manich says, "I reflect on my memories of going to the markets on the east side of Chicago with my grandmother. There was one grocer who remembered everyone's names and what they bought and what they made from what they bought. He would ask someone, 'How long has it been since you made that wonderful stew?'

"Thirty years later I still remember that guy. That's what his grocery stood for."

There's no reason why high-tech companies can't do the same thing today. You can make a conscious decision to support your brand in everything you do. Most marketing experts would agree with Manich that if you stay in a close relationship with your customers, you're most likely going to keep them. You're also going to hang onto market share and continually increase it.

While technology products are first evaluated rationally, they ultimately are chosen on an emotional level. Because of the multitiered purchase process at work within most companies, business product purchases usually follow this two-step selection process: The buyers know what brand they want, then build a rational case for presentation to the purchase approvers. When all the rows and columns of features and specifications are analyzed side by side, the selection between comparable products is made on the strength of the brand.

According to a Cahners Advertising Research Report, nearly

four out of five buyers believe that the reputation of a brand name is as important as the technical specifications of the product. Buyers and specifiers prefer brands because a familiar brand provides good postsale support, substantially reduces the risk of having a buying recommendation rejected, and decreases the risk of disappointment after the sale.[1]

The strongest technology brands, such as HP LaserJet printers, Intel Inside, Apple Macintosh computers, and Microsoft Windows, acknowledge both the intellectual and the emotional aspects of their relationship with their customers, and build on these within the context of a rapidly evolving business environment.

Although, as discussed in Chapter 3, there are substantial differences between consumer and technology markets (and between markets in general), TechnoBranding is the same concept as consumer branding, with a twist. It combines the proven techniques of consumer branding with a deep understanding of the technology customer in order to stimulate buying within a rapidly evolving and complex market. It recognizes and embraces the subtle differences among technology buyers in terms of their expertise, channel choices, and purchase motivations.

Unfortunately, even though the process is understood and known to work, few companies and marketing staffs actually practice it rigorously and reap the benefits of brand development.

Small Is TechnoWonderful

If you're thinking, "TechnoBranding is a great idea, but my company is too small to take advantage of it," this next story is for you. Maxis, a relatively small software company that produces wonderful simulation software, such as Sim City and Sim Life, has demonstrated that you don't need a big advertising budget to make effective use of a strong branding strategy.

There's a tremendous amount of pricing pressure in today's marketplace, pressure that Maxis has responded to creatively. According to Robin Harper, vice president of marketing for Maxis, people are very concerned that they get value when they spend money, whether it's for software, soap, or anything else.

The main question to ask yourself, then, is, "How do I communicate value?" It's a particularly important question when customers aren't familiar with your product. As Harper says, buying software isn't like buying bleach, where you buy the same brand every time.

At Maxis, brand is defined as "an associated image that customers know and have a reaction to." The company realized that its job is to help customers feel that they're getting value for their money. This is especially important for software purchases because people often aren't certain what they're getting.

To create value, Maxis decided to begin by imprinting a positive perception of the brand in the customer's mind. Step two was to focus on developing an expectation that would make customers feel more comfortable about the purchase.

Most companies depend on advertising to create brand awareness, but that requires a relatively large investment; one or two ads simply won't do the job. For a small company like Maxis, spending the amount of money that an ongoing advertising campaign takes simply wasn't possible.

So, given their limited budget, Maxis marketers asked themselves, "How do we maintain effective communication without relying on advertising?" The answer they came up with was that while advertising is very helpful, it isn't the only way to reach your customers. Less expensive communication tools can also be effective.

What to do? Maxis decided to look at other, more cost-efficient means of creating brand awareness. It identified four tools: (1) corporate identity, or recognition of the Maxis name and an association with Maxis that's consistent; (2) public relations; (3) direct marketing; and (4) packaging. In this case history, we cover Maxis's strategies for corporate identity and public relations.

Believing that corporate identity is the foundation for developing a brand, Maxis asked the question, "What do people think of when they think of Maxis?" After conducting consumer research and evaluating the feedback, the company learned that the first key element of its identity is fun, which shows up in two ways. First, Maxis is considered to be irreverent and sometimes silly because its manuals are full of puns and surprises, and goofy jokes are an undercurrent in its games. Second, people have fun playing the games, which generally are challenging, and the company wants to maintain that kind of fun from product to product.

Another key element of the corporate identity is that Maxis stands for sophisticated entertainment. It doesn't produce arcade games, so when people buy a Maxis product, they have an expectation of getting a kind of entertainment they might not find somewhere else.

The company also strives to maintain a position of technology leadership. Maxis's goal in this area is to be on the leading edge with computing power, not necessarily the best graphics and best sound. Although it provides good graphics and sound, it focuses on rendering technologies and artificial life technologies that are at the cutting edge.

Having clarified the company's identity, the marketing communication team then concentrated on maintaining a consistent image throughout all their communications and public relations. Harper adds a cautionary note: You can deliver more than you promise, but you can never deliver less.

The way in which you communicate is also critical. Harper says it helps to think of each piece of communication as the voice of the company. At Maxis, in everything that goes out, whether it's the back-of-the-box copy, an ad, the manuals, or a registration card, the company works hard to maintain the same tone and to communicate with the customers in the same way so that customers begin to get a sense of the company's personality. "The marketing term for this is 'brand character,' and that's what we're trying to achieve," Harper says.

Maxis has used public relations in the same way, using every opportunity to provide the same consistent, focused message—a consistent personality. The brand is always placed in the context of the corporate identity, the corporate personality. The objective is to have everyone in the organization who might be talking to the press speak with one voice.

The way the Maxis marketing communication staff supports that effort is by making sure that everybody in the organization has access to all of the press releases, and by devoting significant amounts of time to developing the right messages that reflect the company personality. While this may be viewed as standard public relations, it's easy to become lax about it; Maxis works hard not to let that happen.

By concentrating on its message development, in fact, it created a term for its products that's been picked up by the press. The term is *software toys*, and because the press has adopted it to refer to Maxis products, it's taken on a special meaning.

The lesson to be learned from the Maxis story is that branding doesn't have to be expensive, but, as Harper concludes, it's "an investment you can make that's absolutely invaluable." Because the marketplace is changing so quickly and so dramatically (particularly in software), with a myriad of options available, the more confidence you can instill in consumers, the more successful you'll be. The industry recognizes the quality of Maxis's marketing; Maxis was winner of the 1993 *Marketing Computers'* third annual Marcom Awards in two categories: new product rollout (software) and packaging.

Consistent, confidence-building communication is far more than making sure your packages look the same on the shelf—it's a way of communicating with your customer. The basic building block is a strong product; branding won't help if the product is a bad one. But if you want to build a business, you've got to get somebody to pick up your product, and then you've got to build a good relationship with the customer.

In children's software alone, there are 2,500 titles, of which 750 are active. The one that's best isn't necessarily going to jump off the shelf. So, for example, if parents know the Sim title, whether it's the package look or the brand name that they remember, then Maxis has an advantage over its competitors.

TechnoBranding: The Six Basic Steps To Build a Strong TechnoBrand

As we've stated, TechnoBranding is a trademarked process, developed by Floathe Johnson, for defining, creating, and managing brand equity for technology-based products and companies. It consists of the following steps:

1. Identify the questions that need to be answered and define the problem(s) to be solved.

2. Conduct qualitative and quantitative research to understand fully who the customers are, how they perceive the brand and competitive brands, and the buying process.
3. Define the brand, which includes positioning, brand associations, brand naming, brand symbol, graphic identity, taglines, and brand personality.
4. Develop a brand strategy and marketing communications plan to apply the brand definition to all customer relationships.
5. Create and execute an integrated marketing communications program.
6. Manage the brand continuously and track it through research to grow, maintain, and leverage brand equity.

Let's look at each step.

Identify the Questions That Need to Be Answered

Sit down and ask, "What are my objectives, what problems need solutions, and what questions need to be answered?" Use these as your guides to decide what research needs to be done and how the TechnoBrand process will evolve. The process described in this book is only one recipe and one model for brand development. It is systematic and it works, but each situation is different.

Conduct Qualitative and Quantitative Research

Research answers questions like:

- What are my customers' perceptions about my company, my products, and my competitors?
- What are the demographics of my customer sets, and what is most important to each set?
- What product attributes and messages are most important when customers are ready to purchase?
- Where are my competitors weak and vulnerable?

The foundation of TechnoBranding is research (discussed more fully in Chapter 5). Many companies ignore this step, assuming that they know the marketplace sufficiently. But after consulting with hundreds of technology companies, we've found that a company's internal view of a market almost never coincides with the real world. This is because there's too much vested interest in the market's being a certain way, rather than the way it is.

You need to understand the deep motivations that drive customer purchase, develop a hypothesis about why people want a relationship with your brand, and then test the hypothesis. Testing, at the least, requires some qualitative audits of the customer, prospect, dealer, editor, and analyst communities. At the other end of the testing spectrum, quantitative research can determine the optimal brand associations and messages, track brand awareness and consideration, and ensure that you aren't unknowingly losing ground on the brand battlefield.

Define the Brand

Defining the brand answers questions like:

- How do we set ourselves apart from and make ourselves seen as better than our competition?
- How can we make it easy for customers to select and purchase our brands?
- How can I get my entire company telling the same story to all customers?

Once customer and market information is gathered through research and situation analysis, the brand definition process takes off from the conclusions. TechnoBrands are defined primarily by positioning and brand associations.

Positioning

Positioning is a process for getting your point of differentiation seen and heard in a crowded marketplace and for establishing a place in your customer's mind that is perceived to be superior to your competitors. Long a mainstay of successful public relations programs, the positioning process helps a company develop a short, one- to two-sentence description of its products' unique benefits. If you articulate, from a customer's point of view, just what problem your product is solving, customers can more easily identify themselves *as* your customers. Here's an example of a positioning statement and then some of the story behind it:

> In an easy, affordable, and fun package, Scan/US combines analysis, data, and map presentation. It is the first business software for geomarket analysis, helping you to make location-related marketing decisions, from the national level down to the neighborhood.

To differentiate itself from mapping software companies, Scan/US defined a new software category, geomarket analysis. Scan/US software transforms numeric spreadsheet data into easy-to-understand, color-keyed maps so that marketing professionals can immediately see where their customers are, quickly change variables, see the results displayed geographically, and present the results or decision criteria to others in an "at-a-glance" format.

"The positioning process made us understand our key marketing messages," explains Ken Needham, president of Scan/US. "It helped us move beyond just ease of use to concentrate upon the fact that the product is really engaging, rewarding, and fun to use. In the past, we brought products to market with a seat-of-the-pants approach, where we really didn't have a sounding board for crystallizing and putting together concepts. This time, we did it in a professional and responsible way, which has really helped us understand and feel confident about our position in the marketplace."

Needham has become a proponent of going through the positioning process. Before they looked at positioning, Scan/US developers said, "These are the features that should be in the product, and we know best." Now, he says, all software developers should get outside help to understand the dynamics of what's being demanded in the marketplace versus the product they want to sell.

Brand Associations: The Buying Triggers

In conjunction with the positioning statement, a company should choose those associations it wants its brand to stand for in the consumer's mind. Associations are how we order what we know about a product or company. These can be either current associations that just need further development or new ones that the company stakes out for itself in the future. Do you think it's just luck that McDonald's is the place children want to go? Carefully crafted associations—Ronald McDonald, Happy Meals, Golden Arches, consistency—have been skillfully embedded in the minds of the youth of America.

The most effective way to communicate brand associations is not in lists, but in nodal maps that are modeled on the way our brain stores and remembers things. In Figure 4-1, the brand name (McDonald's) is placed in an oval in the center of the map, and then each brand association (Golden Arches, Ronald McDonald, Happy Meal) is placed inside an oval called a node and connected to the brand name with a line. Secondary associations (toy, fun) or attributes linked to the primary brand associations are then linked as well. Associations that evoke other associations are linked together, creating networked nodes that graphically depict how customers collectively store images, ideas, and messages about the brand.

The process of developing brand associations can take many forms, including the use of metaphors (if the product were an animal, which would it be?), obituaries (what would someone write in this product's obituary?), and nodal maps to help articulate current and future brand associations. A mixture of emotional and rational associations is best for encouraging buying behavior because, as discussed earlier, people buy for both rational and emotional reasons.

Don't try to put forth more than two or three associations, as they take a long time to develop and most companies do not have the bandwidth or resources to develop more than that number.

Pick associations tied to the purchase decision. Associations can be developed from either concrete aspects (benefits, features) or abstract aspects (emotive intangibles such as logos, characters,

Figure 4-1. Simplified McDonald's nodal map of brand associations.

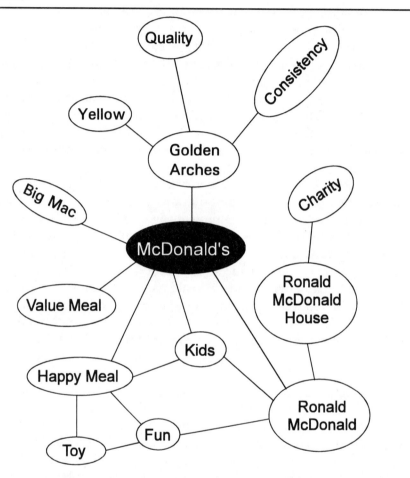

quality, reliability). Abstract associations act as memory shorthand for the company or product and become more important as the market matures.

Develop a Brand Strategy and Marketing Communications Plan

Apply brand to all customer relationships. This helps answer questions like:

- How can we ensure that we become a finalist in the selling cycle?
- What is the best way to communicate and build our brand identity?
- How will we achieve our marketing objectives?
- What is the best mix of marketing communications?
- How can we integrate brand into all customer relationships?

After the positioning and association stage is set, a comprehensive marketing communications plan needs to be created. This plan moves from the position and associations through objectives, strategies, and tactics. Actual implementation of the brand takes place in advertising, public relations, sales promotion, direct marketing, and customer service. Publish a brand identity handbook giving the rules for using the brand internally in order to build and preserve brand equity while still allowing freedom of creative execution at the tactical and project level.

Create and Execute an Integrated Marketing Communications Program

This answers questions like:

- What symbols, names, characters, images, design, and "look and feel" best express our position and brand?

This is the fun part, at least for a lot of people in the advertising business, because this is where the theory and research are actually put to paper or electronic media. This is where the words and pictures that will speak to the customer are created and synthesized into selling art.

Manage the Brand Continuously

"We have not, as a company, historically, been conscious of the importance of managing the overall HP brand," admits Roy Verley, director of corporate communications for Hewlett-Packard Company. He says the company still doesn't fully understand conceptually the elements of branding, brand management, and

TechnoBranding and how they apply to HP. The company hasn't yet determined how best to use the HP brand as a corporate asset and as a leverage point for all HP's business units.

However, HP is committed to quickly spreading the brand knowledge that exists in parts of the company, such as the LaserJet and DeskJet business units, to other units of the company. At the same time, the company is trying to understand what the HP brand itself stands for and what it means to all the HP business entities. Verley expects that, given the change in HP's business, the change in its customer set, and the change in its channels of distribution, some of the traditional associations with HP may be changing, or have already changed.

Traditionally, some of the HP brand associations have been: reliable, high-quality, well managed, and financially stable. Product associations have typically been: high-quality, reliable, indestructible, expensive, and overengineered. However, these associations may or may not still apply, especially as the company moves to aggressively advertising printers and other products at low cost. The HP messages in the marketplace are changing, and the new messages will naturally have an impact on the traditional associations with the company.

As Verley notes, changing the brand without consciously knowing how and why can be dangerous. You need to start by having a good grasp of what the brand stands for, what customers or users derive from the use of the brand, and you need to be very careful not to erode that unless there is an overwhelming reason to do so. Even if you aren't aware of your brand's equity, or what it stands for, it's there, and careless management of it can quickly erode it.

For people looking to manage brand in a large corporation, Verley recommends proceeding with caution: "Don't leap to conclusions about the need to brand things." He explains that at HP, there's been a rush to be contemporary, to recognize that branding is important in high-tech and to immediately assume that that means that everything should be branded. But first there needs to be a real understanding of branding concepts—how to measure brand, how to value it, and how to quantify what level of branding makes sense for individual products, product families, and entire companies. A careful analytical approach needs to be taken, founded on research and a deep conceptual understanding, before launching into a branding effort.

Also keep in mind that TechnoBranding is not just a one-time event. It requires a long-term commitment to the business and a willingness to invest in thoroughly understanding customer behavior.

Tips for Small and Medium-Sized Companies

As the story about Maxis earlier in this chapter shows, brand isn't just the province of large companies. If you're an officer in a small to medium-sized company, practice the basics: Make sure your brand name and logo are consistently and prominently displayed and embed your key brand messages in all communications. You can make a good start with TechnoBranding simply by being consistent in your graphic identity. Here's a simple test. Put all your marketing communication materials on the wall or table. Does your brand name or logo stand out? Or does it look like each piece comes from a different company? Call in your agency or creative department and get their suggestions for creating a consistent image.

Why is brand building important for smaller companies? Chances are your company will be sold or will merge at some point. At that time, the more you have built your brand equity, the more you will get for your stock.

Start Today

Two key steps in TechnoBrand management are: Take the first step today, and continually educate and train people in your company about brand. TechnoBranding is not a quick read or an instant cure. It starts with one person saying, "I think we should apply the TechnoBranding process here."

John Ardussi, marketing manager for ELDEC Corporation, which manufactures airplane electronic products, attended a one-day TechnoBranding course sponsored by the American Electronics Association. He says the seminar made him more aware of the issue. In the aerospace business, branding isn't used much as a marketing tool because parts are custom-made to a customer's specifications. Because it isn't a commodity business, differentiation is often based less on name than on the technical aspect of the product.

Even so, Ardussi thinks branding could be used more extensively at ELDEC because the company is looking outside the aerospace industry for new business. As the company enters new markets, brand issues will become more important.

The power supply business, which is the section of the industry Ardussi is involved with, is a fragmented business. There are hundreds of companies, each with a small market share, so branding could be used to gain significant market presence. However, technology is still a key element in the mix.

"Most companies in our industry are too small to understand branding—or to implement it effectively if they do understand it," Ardussi says. "However, there's a lot of change going on in aerospace markets, and whenever there's change, there's an opportunity to do things differently. The power supply companies that have understood and implemented branding have shown the best growth."

The Intel Brand Campaign

The Intel Inside program was one of the first brand campaigns in the technology industry and is still the most visible. "Intel Inside" defuses Intel clone vendors, creates pull for Intel-based computers (gets computer buyers to seek out Intel-powered computers), and enables premium-brand pricing for both the ingredient (the computer chip) and the end-user program. The theme is upgradability, and the message is that having an Intel processor inside a PC means state-of-the-art technology and helps the consumer protect his or her computer investment.

The total amount spent on the campaign is a matter for speculation. The best estimates are $250 million for the second half of 1991 and 1992, with over half coming from co-op partners. It certainly is the most expensive ad campaign ever launched by a semiconductor company.

By way of background, in a May 1991 court ruling, "386" became common nomenclature; Intel could no longer prevent other companies from using it as a product name. Faced with this, Intel needed to find a way to highlight Intel products and not those of its competitors. At the time, Intel had a small logo program in Japan called "Intel In It" that was very similar in look to the current Intel Inside logo. Out of this "crisis" came the decisions to trademark the Intel Inside logo and to embark on a brand advertising campaign that expanded marketing beyond Intel's traditional OEM customers to include end users.

Prior to the Intel Inside brand campaign, the company had successfully talked directly to end users about microprocessors once before, according to Ken Rutsky, manager of microprocessor brand strategy at Intel Corporation. It happened in 1991, when Intel had an entry-level 386-class product called the i386SX microprocessor. Even though the i386SX was very close in price to the older 286 and offered much greater performance, the market was slow to adopt it.

Intel responded by running what it called the Red X campaign, which was basically a billboard and print advertising campaign that featured a spray-painted red X over the number 286; next to it on the billboard, or on the second page of the ad, was the number 386SX. Intel didn't call it brand then, but the Red X campaign created 386SX as a brand and was very effective in creating pull to 386 products rather than 286 products. The success of the campaign, which earned very high recognition, was one of the factors that led to the decision to go with the Intel Inside program.

One of the first Intel inside ads, shown in Figure 4-2, was a simple two-page spread. This is branding with a hammer, associating quality with a brand and logo. Simple message. Simple visual. Repeated over and over, in everything from ads to posters to TV commercials, and especially in all the ads of the computer manufacturers who use Intel microprocessors. All with the goal of having computer buyers associate the best computers with Intel Inside.

The objectives of the Intel Inside program are constant worldwide: to create awareness of and preference for the Intel brand of microprocessors among end users, to move the market to the next level of performance, and to raise the demand for Intel processing

(*text continues on page 74*)

Figure 4-2. Intel Inside advertisement.

How to spot the ve

ry best computers.

It's really quite easy. From notebooks to mainframes, just look for computers that have a genuine Intel microprocessor inside. Either the Intel386,™ Intel386 SX, Intel386 SL, Intel486™ or Intel486 SX microprocessor.

Intel is the world's leader in microprocessor design and development. And no other microprocessors have a larger installed base of software. Plus, every chip is literally put through millions of tests. So with Intel inside, you know you've got unquestioned compatibility and unparalleled quality. Or simply put, the very best computer technology.

So look for the Intel Inside symbol on ads for leading computers. Or call 800-548-4725. It'll show you've got an eye for spotting the best.

intel.

The Computer Inside.™

Source: Intel Corporation.

power. Awareness and preference are measured by extensive brand research on Intel microprocessors among the specified purchasers of PCs and some other audiences. "Among our target markets, we have achieved very high levels of awareness," Rutsky says.

While Intel's objectives of building awareness and preference and selling "more performance" are constant worldwide, ingredient brand licensing programs are tailored by market. An ingredient brand, such as Intel's microprocessor chips, is a brand that is not directly purchased by the consumer. NutraSweet is a familiar consumer example.

There are some special challenges that come with being a technology brand and an ingredient brand at the same time. For example, with NutraSweet, the end user doesn't care about the formulation or specifications; the product is either the right sweetness or not. With microprocessors, a lot of the technical change can translate into greater performance for the end user, which is something the end user cares about. Explaining that to end users can be very difficult, but is also very important.

There are two parts to the Intel Inside program: the print merchandising program and the point-of-purchase merchandising program. Both are cooperative marketing programs. "Our customers use the Intel Inside logo in their print advertising as well as on their shipping cartons, their actual system unit, and their point-of-purchase merchandising material," Rutsky explains. "Because we are in a global market, with a lot of people manufacturing their machines in one country and shipping them worldwide, we transitioned to 100 percent Intel Inside and discontinued Intel In It. It's better for our customers to have a consistent program worldwide."

The Intel Inside campaign is an example of the brand relationship-building approach. By using consistent words and pictures in a variety of media, both Intel and its OEM computer customers reinforce the positive brand relationship that the computer industry and consumers have with the Intel brand. Intel ads help customers understand that when they've got Intel microprocessors inside their PC, they've got the authentic article and are assured of compatibility. And Intel's main competitor, Advanced Micro Devices, can't put the Intel Inside brand and Pentium, the first nonnumerical brand name for an Intel microprocessor, on its chips.

As an article in *High-Tech Marketing News* stated,

> Branding technology as a term may itself be an oxymoron, suggested Karen Alter, manager of brand public relations at Intel, "because technology changes so quickly and can be complicated."
>
> Nonetheless, "Intel Inside" is TechnoBranding. "We use it because technology does move fast and is complicated," she said. The challenge is to make shoppers into buyers. "We know more and more people are buying tech products in mass channels, places where they traditionally haven't gone to buy that equipment. That means anything that can simplify their decision is really useful, and that's what a brand does," said Alter.
>
> A name like Pentium provides a way to create a unique product name while also making it easy for consumers to find the product. "We can explain why it's good but you have to have a kind of shorthand of why that product has benefits for the consumer," she said. Intel will continue its shift from nomenclature to names "when it's meaningful."[2]

Brand names are very valuable corporate assets. Why make it easy for competitors to copy your product and capitalize on your hard-earned technological advantage? To name the "586" microprocessor, Intel hired a firm specializing in names, asked employees for suggestions, and began getting lots of unsolicited names. Over 3,300 suggestions were reviewed to come up with the name Pentium. Why was it chosen? Pentium is a protectable trademark, and it is not offensive in other languages. The *pent* of Pentium comes from the Greek, meaning "five," alluding to the fifth generation of the X86 family.

Figure 4-3 is an example of a map showing how Intel might define its brand. Branching off the brand name Intel are the key attributes that customers and the public think of when they think "Intel." Linked to these attributes are secondary associations that are linked and networked together in people's memory.

Figure 4-3. Intel nodal map of brand associations.

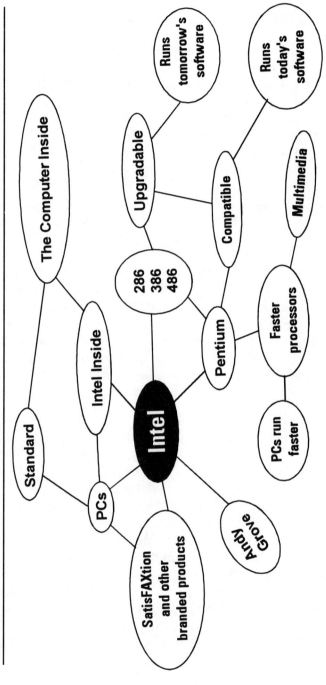

How Does TechnoBranding Get Results?

Figure 4-4 summarizes how TechnoBrands are built to get results. On the far left and right sides, we see the short- and long-term desired results: sales and brand equity, respectively. Brand equity yields increased corporate net worth, stock value, loyalty, and profits.

TechnoBrands bridge the gap between short-term sales and long-term brand equity by identifying customer needs and motivations, particularly at the time of purchase. These buying triggers are defined as positioning and brand association messages and targeted to market segments, specific customer groups, to effectively differentiate the brand from competitive brands. The result of this TechnoBranding step is the development of a network of psychological persuaders and emotional buying triggers.

These key messages and impressions are useless unless customers recognize them and relate to them in their minds and hearts. Therefore, they need to be creatively expressed and dramatized in the form of memorable messages and regular news to keep the brand alive and fresh. The result is a proprietary visual, emotional image and personality.

Ultimately, we want to change customers' perceptions and buying behavior to the point where they think, "I need a printer. I want an HP LaserJet printer." If you want something from someone, keep repeating and telling them what you want. Condition your customers to purchase your brand by repeating the brand messages and proprietary visual and emotional images through integrated marketing communications, including advertising, public relations, and, ideally, all customer contact with the brand.

In a world in which technology companies are learning to cannibalize their own products before competitors do, one of the greatest benefits of brand is the contribution it makes to the stockholder value of a company. Think of TechnoBranding as a brand lifestyle to ensure long life and prosperity.

How Much Is Enough?

A key question asked by many high-tech executives is how much to spend on product advertising and brand advertising. This ques-

Figure 4-4. How TechnoBranding works.

Short-term result = sales	→ Recognition & affinity →	Behavioral conditioning →	Long-term result = brand equity
Needs & motivations	Get in their minds/hearts	Consistency & repetition	Net worth
Reasons to buy	Creative expression	Integrated marketing communications	Stock value
Positioning + associations	Proprietary visual or emotional image or personality	Stimulus + response = conditioned behavior—"I need a printer. I want an HP LaserJet."	Loyalty
Segmentation & differentiation	Memorable positive messages & impressions		Profits
Development of a network of psychological persuaders & emotional triggers	Regular news		

tion is misguided; since customers buy brands (even in technology markets), *all* advertising expenditures should be spent on brand advertising.

The real question is the supposed trade-off between advertising to achieve short-term sales and advertising to build long-term brands. In fact, as shown in Figure 4-4, the trade-off is not as great as envisaged.

If the advertising communicates the brand values, it is likely to be more effective in facilitating a sale in the short term among purchasers currently in the market for the product concerned. For example, associations such as ergonomic or intuitive factors are more likely to influence specific market segments, and thus differentiate the advertiser, than "486" or "eight megabytes RAM," which merely claim membership in the market in general. The craft of good advertising is to develop the right creative interpretation of these brand values and apply them over the long term, creating the equity that can make all forms of communication work more effectively.

Adopt TechnoBrand Management

Consider assigning the role of TechnoBrand managers rather than product managers or even marketing communications managers. Brand managers are rarely found in high-tech companies. They should be.

In any case, the changing market does not make brand management easy. Even in technology markets, with largely compatible products, it is recognized that product values have largely given way to competitive values. In the world of technology, the biggest competitors are often a company's biggest allies.

Brand values not only differentiate a company and its products, they place it above the competition, or even create a new category. From financing the purchase to the friendliness of the receptionist, companies need to look at the broad scope of values (as opposed to only product values) being purchased. The future lies with companies that can fully utilize this concept and fully integrate the TechnoBrand associations into every aspect of the company's service to the customer.

Notes

1. "How Important Is the Reputation of a Brand Name?" Cahners Advertising Research Report No. 120.13, undated.
2. Art Garcia, "Market Changes Make Brand Building Critical," *High-Tech Marketing News*, CMP Publications, Inc., July/August 1993, 21. Used by permission.

5

The Absolute Importance Of Research

"You can't know too much about the needs, the interests, and the expectations of your customers and those of your competitors."

Dave Roberts, worldwide advertising manager
Claris Corporation

There is an old saying that companies use research like a drunk uses a lamppost—for support rather than illumination.

The purpose of research is simple: to achieve dominant awareness and loyalty by representing "the voice of the customer." By systematically developing a deep understanding of the customer, managers simplify decisions and maximize the probability of success. Applied to TechnoBranding, research starts with what's in the customer's mind, then strengthens the bond between brand and buyer. The goal is *not* to manipulate in an Orwellian sense or to create pseudobrands. Rather, the goal is to bring the customer everything he or she wants and expects in the brand.

Many high-tech companies perceive research as generating reams of data for research's sake only and lacking any practical use. Yet companies put extraordinary amounts of effort into improving product quality, then refuse to put the same amount of effort into understanding what quality means to customers.

Research goes beyond what consumers think or do. To truly understand customers, we need to know what their conscious, rational selves want. We need to understand their emotional needs, their psychological and spiritual needs, and the cultural and status-related values that influence them in making decisions. (Indeed, the leading brands of tomorrow will be developed with the help of psychologists, cultural anthropologists, and perhaps even spiritual leaders.) Then, we can build brands that mirror and reinforce those values. From there, "news is the oxygen that allows existing brands to breathe, live and grow."[1]

Know the Customer

Research is neither a magical cure nor a curse. It is a practical brand marketing tool to help you know your customer. Here is a checklist to help you decide when and when not to use research.
Use research when:

- There is a hypothesis worth testing.
- You lack information needed to make a clear decision.
- You are weighing alternatives.
- There is a conflict in the organization on the direction to take.
- You need to hear the voice of the customer in order to make company or market critical decisions.

Don't use research when:

- You honestly know enough to make a decision.
- Good secondary information already exists.
- The research is not projectable or performable.
- The cost exceeds the projected payoff.

"The challenge is when to use research and when to use judgment," says Derrith Lambka, corporate advertising manager for Hewlett-Packard. "Totally depending on research is very risky because customers oftentimes won't tell you a lot of things they're dealing with that are emotional and irrational, and so they may tell you one thing and act another way." To deal with this problem, track both the customers' attitudes and their behavior. Then, compare the two.

Strive to have a continual discussion with customers in the marketplace so that you know what's happening. Lambka says the customers for on-line services and new interactive media are very important for technology companies because on-line users have got to be really computer savvy to know how to maneuver through the system. Often, these are the power users and influencers that other people go to for answers on what to buy.

"It all comes back to know the customer, know the customer, know the customer," Lambka states. And know that the customer is also going to be changing.

TechnoBranding facilitates the shift from push to pull orientation. In "the good old days," you could push out with lots of literature, advertising, and the hard sell, requiring the customers to cope and try to figure out what they wanted. That's not going to be the case in the future as people come to expect personalized marketing and experience the shift from a one-way street to not only a two-way street, but a multilane information highway. Companies will have to continually reengineer themselves to better meet the needs of customers.

"That's why I'd much rather be in a technology company than work for Jolly Green Giant beans," says Lambka. "What do you say about beans? Beans don't change that much, where our industry changes constantly." The trick is to know the customers, figure out what they want, and figure out a better way to get them the information they want when, where, and how they want it. If you can do that, then branding decisions are an obvious outcome.

Research tests and verifies hunches; it does not create them. Asking the right questions is critical when planning the research project and when creating survey questionnaires, discussion guides, and usability or taste-type tests. Look at the mess Coke stirred up with New Coke because of blind taste tests. Were consumers asked if they wanted a new Coke?

Research helps management see the brand through the eyes of the customer. Too often, there are differences between what management thinks customers think and what customers really think. When marketing consultant Edward Tauber did a study for

Carnation, he found that management saw Carnation as a large multiproduct company and a leader in food technology. To customers, Carnation simply meant canned milk. In a similar study for Duracell, Tauber's research showed that management thought of its products as consumer electronics. Consumers thought Duracell made flashlights, not electronic products like Sony.[2]

Managers traditionally see themselves as the visionary force behind the company's success. Their jobs demand that they be optimistic and take the company beyond the present. Because they are so involved with the company, they may lose contact with how customers see the company.

When marketers sit behind the one-way mirrors watching customer focus groups talk about companies, one fact comes through over and over: Customers want simple, straightforward messages. Too often the words that turn management on are the words that turn customers off.

The same holds true for engineers and programmers who believe they have designed the best product possible. Put those engineers behind the one-way mirror of the focus group and let them watch customers use and talk about the product they so carefully designed. It can be a humbling experience. Yet, the changes customers suggest are often easy and fast to make and result in dramatic improvements in customers' perceptions of product usability.

Start with What You Can Afford

Research doesn't have to be expensive. Even small companies can conduct surveys on a regular basis. Customer satisfaction studies are one of the best places to start. Current customers provide you with feedback on product performance, why they bought your brand over another, how knowledgeable the dealer or salesperson was, and how the company can improve its products and services. If you have a new product, prospective customers generally appreciate being asked about new product ideas.

What if your competitors already do this kind of research? If they do, shouldn't you? If they don't, isn't this a smart way to get a competitive edge?

One easy and excellent way to understand your customers is to set up a customer registration system. This can be as easy as including marketing questions on warranty or registration cards included with each product. The benefits are many. You can:

- Build your customer database and mailing list. Your in-house customer database will outpull purchased lists. Use your list for selling upgrades and cross-selling other products. You can even have a list broker rent your list to other noncompetitive companies and earn add-on revenue, while the broker maintains and updates the list for you.
- Gather customer segmentation and demographic data. Find out customers' company SIC (Standard Industrial Classification) code, title, function, as well as their age, income, and location, if that is relevant.
- Ask customers questions about their decision to purchase your product, where they bought the product, and their recommendations for improving your service to them.
- Find out why they bought your product and their satisfaction or dissatisfaction with it.

Warranty cards are an inexpensive and effective means to find out what product attributes (potential brand associations) are linked to product purchase. Depending on the product, registration may be as low as 20 percent or as high as 40 percent for more technical hardware or software.

One small manufacturing company, Heart Interface, asks customers to check off the two factors that most influenced their product purchase. From the data, three factors rose above all others. Heart Interface followed up with a customer satisfaction survey to learn how these factors ranked and why. This kind of information helps focus marketing communications on the messages that turn prospects into customers.

Again, this is not research for research's sake. The purpose is to find ways to improve customer satisfaction, increase the chances of new product success, determine exactly why customers buy from you, gather timely competitive information, and measure the effectiveness of marketing and communications.

Ask Questions before Beginning

Before deciding what kind of research to do, define the problem and research objectives. Think through what questions you really need to have answered. Here are some questions that will help you do this:

- Why are you conducting the research?
- How are you going to use the information?
- What do you need to know and what would you like to know? Is there anything in the "need to know" category that should be in the "like to know" category?
- Is any of the information available from a secondary source, research already done and publicly available (the research library, industry publications, industry research tracking studies, on-line data searches, etc.)?
- When do you need it?
- How much detail is needed?
- Will this study serve as a benchmark that will be periodically replicated?
- How much is the information worth?

Primary Qualitative and Quantitative Research

There are two basic types of primary (customized) research: qualitative and quantitative.

Qualitative research seeks to understand the qualities and characteristics of a small group of subjects. To understand this "critical few," focus groups, advisory boards, and one-on-one interviews are used to gather "soft" responses on opinions, perceptions, and attitudes. This type of research is simple, quick, and inexpensive. Use it carefully when you want to test an opinion, message content and impact, or creative concept, or to verify an instinct. Don't use it when you need the data to be projectable to the entire market.

Quantitative research seeks to know that the gathered data will be projectable to the entire target audience. A statistically significant sample of the entire audience ("the useful many") is polled, using mail surveys, telephone surveys, data panels, or personal interviews, to gather hard data. Use this type of research when you need to be right on target, when the risks warrant the investment, when the information is strategically significant to company success, and when specific or highly technical alternatives need to be weighed.

Data panels, offered by research firms such as Techtel, provide companies with a pool of prescreened target audience subjects for quick studies (e.g., market share data, conversion-to-sales data). Questionnaires are faxed to the panel, with responses returned in a few days via fax and 800 numbers. The call-ins leave their responses by using a Touch-Tone phone; they can also leave recorded comments, which are often as useful as the data itself.

Start with qualitative research to elicit key dimensions of the brand and purchase choice criteria: the long list of attributes, needs, wants, and deficiencies. Then use quantitative research to validate and rank the most important attributes and segment the market.

TechnoBranding Qualitative Study

The first steps toward brand relationship marketing are (1) a situation analysis, (2) a communications audit, (3) an initial qualitative study ("soft soundings") of customers, magazine editors and newspaper reporters, and management, followed by (4) positioning and brand association research and development. The positioning and brand associations should be checked in a focus group.

The *situation analysis* includes an evaluation of the company goals and expectations; the marketing objectives; a SWOT (strengths, weaknesses, opportunities, and threats) analysis; perceptions of the market infrastructure (editors, analysts, investors); and a discussion of the products, markets, target audiences, competition, pricing, and distribution channels.

The *communications audit* has a number of purposes: to take a "snapshot" of the advertising and business environment; to analyze communications program effectiveness on a cost/benefit basis; to compare competitors' messages, positions, and brand associations with the company's; and to identify ways to improve the performance of the communications program. This is done by collecting copies of all existing communications materials, plans, and budgets; collecting data summarizing the results of previous communications programs; gathering published information on competitors; reviewing available research; researching ad spending levels; and creating a "war room" to evaluate and analyze all information in context.

All materials are reviewed in the context of the company's overall marketing and communication goals. Do they appear to be achieving the stated objectives? How do spending levels compare? What is the current mix of advertising, trade shows, public relations, and direct marketing? How should the mix be changed? How could the company's positioning and brand associations be better integrated into communications materials?

The *qualitative study,* or soft soundings, offers a cost-effective means to define the brand. Soft soundings consist of a series of interviews with customers, prospects, lost customers, editors, channel members (e.g., dealers), and analysts, and face-to-face interviews with company management. Soft soundings provide a quick and relatively inexpensive way to get the pulse of the market by asking questions about market trends, benefits, differentiators, and competitors. Their purpose is to get a qualitative glimpse of the market's perceptions and to unearth new information or pitfalls, while providing raw fodder for TechnoBrand definition.

One of the groups interviewed in the qualitative study deserves a fuller explanation. At the center of the high-tech industry lie several "key influencer" groups whose job it is to track changes and forecast trends on a daily basis. These analysts and consultants, who are among the best-kept secrets of corporate success, study and report on trends and opportunities in all major high-tech industry segments. Their influence helps determine which products and technologies succeed and which do not.

On a daily basis, research firms like International Data Corporation and Dataquest compile reams of industry statistics. Analysts and consultants integrate that data into their industry reports, market growth projections, newsletters, stock recommendations, and custom consulting services. A variety of audiences use these reports: companies looking for a competitive edge, investors making buy and sell decisions, and reporters writing about trends, companies, products, and people.

The number of analysts and consultants following any one industry is small relative to their influence. By calling up several of these highly informed sources and asking for their perceptions of your company, your competition, and market trends, you not only tap into their expertise, but you also provide them with information that is vital to them. You can take soft soundings a step further and build a relationship with a network of analysts who know you, favor you, and talk about you to editors and their clients, who usually are the large Fortune 500 corporations.

Using Focus Groups to Test Positioning And Brand Associations

Test. Test. Test. I can't overemphasize the importance of continual customer testing to avoid mistakes in message selection and TechnoBrand definition. More and more companies use focus group research for their market planning and for explorative research. A focus group brings a group of eight to twelve carefully screened people together in a conference room that has a one-way mirror at one end so that the focus group sponsors can see and hear what the target audiences have to say. A moderator, following a discussion guide, asks questions and facilitates discussions about the topics that need to be explored. The focus group moderator plays an important role by managing the interaction within the group and doing things like preventing strong individuals from dominating and skewing the feedback of the group. Focus groups are a relatively fast and inexpensive way to verify that the brand definition is on the right track. Since later advertising and public relations will repeat the positioning and brand associations over and over again, it is important to make sure that they are credible and effective with real customers.

Focus groups are a good way to check a communications concept to determine if anything is confusing, misleading, or negative, and to unearth people's level of understanding and their psychological "hot buttons." However, focus group results are not statistically projectable and should not be used by themselves to make a "go" or "no-go" decision.

TechnoBranding Quantitative Study

The second part of TechnoBranding research is to quantify brand awareness, which includes studying consideration and purchase-influencing messages to validate and profile the target audiences; profiling the purchase process, the buying cycle, and key purchase influencers; measuring what percentage of the target market is aware of the brand; tracking the rankings of the attributes found to be most important in the purchase decision; and determining which attributes are deficient in current offerings.

Your first quantitative study establishes the standard against which the success of brand strategy and marketing communications can be measured. Important follow-up studies measure awareness, consideration, and loyalty, as well as perception and attitudinal changes over time.

Typical quantitative TechnoBrand research falls into two categories, demand-side and supply-side, as shown in Figure 5-1. Demand-side refers to the customer's buying process (moving from awareness through consideration and purchase to loyalty). The number of prospective customers or percentage of market decreases in each step as customers identify their needs, select categories, evaluate options, try out a small number of brands, and finally begin using and reusing the product.

Supply-side refers to the product development cycle: moving from R&D through design, marketing, and manufacturing to sales. The number of final product choices decreases as the company makes technology, product specification, market research, and positioning decisions. Brand associations, marketing and communications, and brand tracking take the product to the customer for consideration.

Each of these steps should be reviewed to see if research can help increase the percentage of the market that will consider and purchase the product, leading to happy customers and a profitable business. TechnoBrand research helps bridge customer needs and company-supplied solutions. Now let's look at the two types of quantitative research: demand-side research and supply-side research.

Figure 5-1. Areas for research and planning during the buying and TechnoBranding processes.

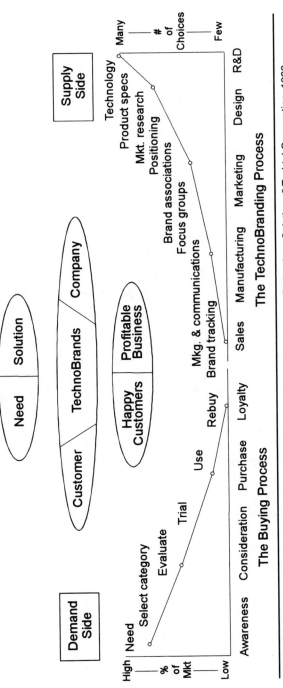

Source: Based on a chart by Michael F. Kelly, "CT Market: How We Find and Use Technology Solutions," Techtel Corporation, 1993.

Demand-Side Research

Demand-side research will help you understand the buying process. In Chapter 2, on the basis of extensive research, we distilled the computer product buying process to three key phases—awareness, consideration, and purchase of a brand. Figure 5-2 helps explain the dynamics of this process. Let's look at some of the phases and processes in depth.

Awareness and Consideration

You need to know how many buyers are aware of your brand compared to your competitors, and what percentage of those buyers include your brand in their consideration set or short list of vendors. You also need to track levels of awareness and consideration. You can conduct primary research (quantitative research surveys of the market) yourself or, if you're in the computer industry, look into the kinds of omnibus services provided by research firms like IntelliQuest and Techtel, which track factors such as the level of unaided brand awareness, the percentage of buyers considering your brand, the percentage of people having an opinion of your brand, and other baseline awareness information. This type of research is fundamental to brand marketing and basic to success.

Unaided brand awareness research asks the question, "When you think of (insert product category), what brands come to mind?" It's important because it allows you to track the order in which brands are remembered so that you can identify the dominant and top-of-mind brands, as well as all brands recalled. Aided brand awareness research lists brand names in the product category and asks which brands the respondent recognizes. While unaided awareness is most important, aided awareness is also helpful when exploring perceptions of competitors that may not be top of mind with buyers or when you want to find out what competitive brands a buyer may have considered in a past purchase.

Brand awareness is important in all technology-based markets, not just computer markets. However, each market is at a different stage of brand "evolution," and these differences must be taken into account. Let's look at the health care market as an example.

Figure 5-2. The dynamics of awareness, consideration, purchase, and loyalty.

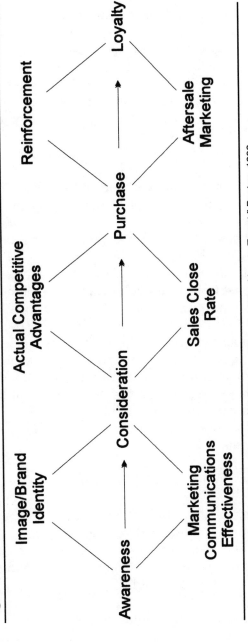

Source: Adapted from International Data Group, "Buying I.T. in the '90s: How to Target," Boston, 1993.

"Brand is important in the awareness portion of the ultra-sound equipment purchase cycle, but becomes less important in the final selection process," says John Konsin, director of market-ing for Advanced Technology Laboratories (ATL). In this market, the customer's brand preference is not always the same as the final brand selection. In the final selection process, customers weigh the importance of price, image quality, technology, and other im-portant product attributes.

Konsin thinks brand will be a much more important factor for success in the future because in the professional health care marketplace, more people will become involved in the purchase process. Successful companies in this market over the past five years have not only offered a superior product, but also positioned their product to targeted customers. If you do a good job managing your brand, you'll build the right image and position in the cus-tomer's mind and be more successful.

For the past three years, ATL has done an annual quality sur-vey of ultrasound purchasers to monitor how ATL is perceived relative to the competition in terms of brand awareness and recog-nition of competitive taglines. In the near future, Konsin predicts, better industry tracking information will become available, en-abling individual companies and products to track how they are doing relative to other companies. "It hasn't been lucrative in the past," Konsin predicts, "but I think the ultrasound industry will be ready to pay for an omnibus tracking study within the next eighteen months."

Image and Brand Identity

Marketing communications efforts aimed at creating and pro-moting a position and brand identity are essential to gaining place-ment of a brand in the buyer's typically small consideration set. Here are some types of brand image to think about that may be important to identify and quantify:

- Product and company image: What beliefs do customers have about the functional and intangible characteristics of the product? How is the product image affected by the com-pany image, and how can it be leveraged?

- User image: What types of people are most likely to buy this product? How do customers in the target market respond to that image?
- Channel image: What are retailers, distributors, and other channel intermediaries looking for, and how can they be motivated to move the product?
- Occasion image: What impressions and images does the customer have about the times and occasions when the brand is used or consumed?
- Brand personality: If the brand was a famous person, animal, or car, what would it be? If the brand was a real person, what kind of personality traits would it have? What did the brand look like five years ago versus today? What could or should the brand look like?
- Salience: What stands out from customers' past, present, and future (fantasy) experiences with the brand, how strongly do they feel about it (emotional closeness or distance), and how inclined are they to buy or try it?[3]

Actual Competitive Advantages

Converting consideration to purchase requires evidence that the product delivers the attributes promised and does so in a manner superior to that of competitive offerings. This can and should be quantified by asking customers and noncustomers to rank the importance of company or product brand attributes and advantages.

Brand Loyalty

Brand-loyal buyers automatically include their current brand in the consideration set—often by itself—when planning their next purchase. This can be measured in customer satisfaction surveys, warranty or registration card statistics, and general market research surveys, such as those done by trade magazines for their advertisers. Marketing communications' task is to reinforce loyalty, to keep the brand's hold on these profitable customers who are willing to pay a price premium and do not require the costly marketing effort needed to generate awareness.

Compaq and the Importance of Consideration

If you aren't tracking consideration levels for both your own brand and your competitors', the following story should change your mind about the importance of doing so. Between mid-1988 and the end of 1991, Compaq dropped 50 percent in consideration—from a level of 16 percent to less than 8 percent, according to Techtel Corporation's PC/Market Opinion research—and the decline continued even when advertising expenditures increased significantly. When spending is going up and consideration is falling, you know you've got a problem; something needs to change.

"Opinion of the brand was falling because of the price," according to Michael Kelly, president of Techtel Corporation, an Emeryville, California–based research firm that specializes in end-user research on high-tech products and companies. In the period from 1988 to the beginning of 1991, the percentage of people with a positive opinion of Compaq dropped from 96 percent to 84 percent. Compaq stayed at a premium price level that was too high for too long; the world had moved on. Computer buyers' perception of the competition was, "It may not be as good as Compaq, but it's good enough for me to save X amount of money."

Figure 5-3, which was developed by Techtel, is a powerful illustration of how research can help a company avoid such a precipitous fall. The chart indicates the percentage of companies considering a purchase of Compaq computer products (all the major products in the line). The numbers on the bottom of the chart indicate each quarter for the years 1988 through 1992.

Three periods are of particular interest. First, from 1988 through 1989, the level of consideration remained around 12 to 14 percent. Then it went through a downtrend period, the most severe part of which was between the second quarter of 1990 and the first quarter of 1991. Consideration hit a flat period in 1991 and early 1992.

What was happening in terms of advertising spending during that same period? "What you're really looking for," Kelly says, "is relations between changes in one measurement and the other one." For example, advertising spending went down during the third quarter of 1988, but consideration went up to the 16 percent level.

During that quarter, Compaq made a major product announcement (the SLT), and the resultant publicity and articles

Figure 5-3. Compaq consideration history.

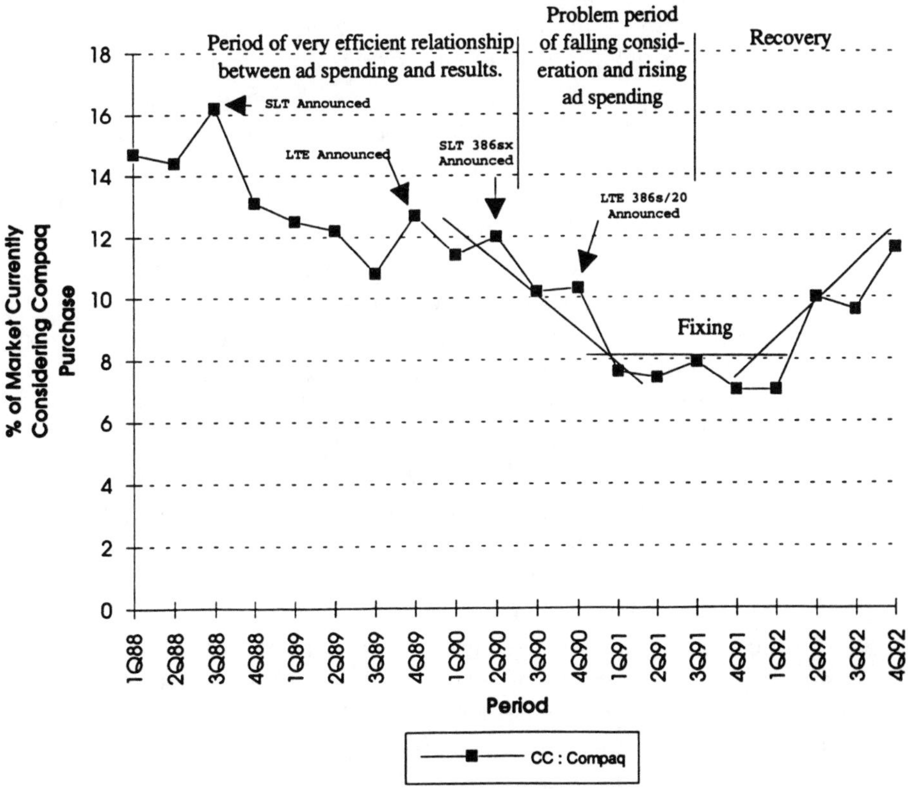

combined with the market's very high opinion of Compaq at the time increased the consideration level.

The announcement of a new product from a company with a high opinion rating allows a cutback on advertising while the company uses public relations to build brand awareness. Editors know that the market wants to know about everything new from leading companies.

During the third quarter of 1988, Compaq spent about half its advertising dollars on television commercials to get the word out about the new product, then it cut TV off and put the money back into print advertising. The strategy was to reach those people who had seen the TV ad but hadn't acted on it, so that when they learned a little more by reading about the product, they would find it interesting enough to want to see it.

The first time this strategy was employed, it was very effective. However, subsequent new product announcements (the LTE product in the fourth quarter of 1989, the SLT 386sx in the second quarter of 1990, and the LTE 386s/20 in the fourth quarter of 1990) had less and less impact each time over the previous level of consideration. During early 1991, Compaq increased advertising spending, but consideration continued downward.

"In the third quarter of 1991, Compaq realized they needed to do something, and the company took steps," Kelly says. "They fired the president, fired their advertising agency, laid off 1400 employees, and took a $70 million loss. They then proceeded to correct the problems and began building on the latent brand opinion, which was still there." Compaq lowered prices and put the emphasis back on better products for more segments. A Compaq press conference around this time announced, "Here's what we recognized our problems to be, and here's what we're doing about it."

By the second quarter of 1992, Compaq not only had fixed things, but it also had raised advertising spending to more than $16 million, and that immediately started to increase consideration. "They were rebuilding the brand, but repositioning it; instead of the brand standing for good quality at a high price, they kept the high quality but replaced the high price with value pricing and broadened from a technology-driven image to customer-driven. That's why they were able to rebuild so fast. People were still ranking those things highly," Kelly says.

Because Compaq had failed to adapt to changing market conditions, positive opinion had fallen. Compaq recovered by fixing its internal problems, emphasizing traditional strengths, keeping Compaq as the core brand name with a family of subbrands like ProLinea and Presario ("A Compaq product for all customers and price points"[4]), focusing on customer needs, and communicating the new message: "Compaq is now value priced."

Measuring Brand Consideration

Measuring brand consideration is complex because it involves studying the choices, beliefs, and perceptions involved in purchase. The basic idea is to track consideration levels for the brand

and its competitors to determine which choices are preferred by customers. Some research tactics for measuring consideration include omnibus research services, customer surveys to understand the purchase process (the buying cycle and decision process), shelf audits, and office or home office visits after customer purchase to understand how the product is actually installed and used. Also helpful are the use of laddering techniques to rank product feature and buyer selection attributes, the use of discrete choice analysis (buyers have to choose between one product/feature/price set and another) to measure price and feature trade-offs, and surveys and focus groups to learn about and define brand image.

Understanding and Researching Brand Loyalty

Understanding the brand loyalty of buyers is essential to making informed and efficient marketing decisions. You can research loyalty through customer satisfaction surveys and switching analysis, which will tell you why customers switch away, why competitors' customers switch to your brand, and what kinds of competitors' customers would be most profitable to move to your brand.

In November 1993, IDG released "Buying I.T. in the '90s: How to Target," the fourth in its series of Buying I.T. reports, which introduces a profit-based market segmentation model. Using this model, marketing and marketing communications professionals can array customers and noncustomers along a brand loyalty continuum and draw implications for developing messages and allocating dollars to the appropriate targets.

The first step for a company implementing IDG's profit-based segmentation model is to generate a brand loyalty matrix like the one provided for Lotus 1-2-3 in Figure 5-4. This matrix divides spreadsheet purchasers surveyed in the "How to Target" research into Lotus customers and non-Lotus customers (along the y axis), then subdivides these clusters on the basis of their relative brand loyalty (along the x axis). Relative brand loyalty is defined by responses to the survey question, "If you were purchasing a spreadsheet again today, how likely would you be to buy the same brand that you last purchased?" On a scale of 1 to 9, where 1 means "not at all likely" and 9 means "very likely," buyers rating 1 to 3 are

Figure 5-4. Brand loyalty matrix: Lotus 1–2–3.

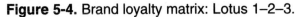

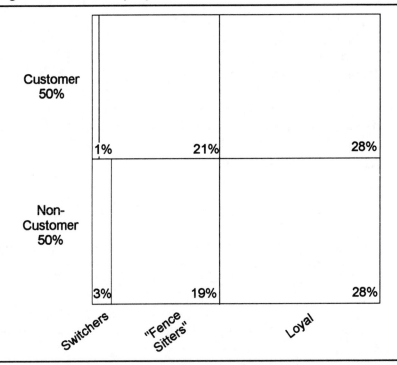

Source: International Data Group, "Buying I.T. in the '90s: How to Target," Boston, 1993, p. 65.

grouped into the switcher category, those rating 4 to 8 are classified as fence sitters, and those rating 9 are called loyal.

In Figure 5-4, we see that Lotus owns 50 percent of the spreadsheet market, and that more than half of its customers are brand loyal. However, its remaining customers—22 percent of the market—would consider abandoning Lotus in their next spreadsheet purchase. In addition, another 22 percent of the market consists of non-Lotus customers who are considering abandoning their current brand. In all, 44 percent of spreadsheet customers are "up for grabs" as they move toward their next purchase.[5]

Combined with other information gained from IDG's research, this matrix can be replicated through your own custom research to answer questions such as:

- What separates my loyal customers from my fence sitters and switchers in terms of what they are looking for in a brand?
- Are there any brands with a disproportionate share of nonloyal customers that I can target?
- Should my marketing messages differ for my own nonloyal customers and those of my competitors?
- Which group of nonloyal customers—my own or my competitors'—more closely matches the profile of my loyal customers?

The answers to questions like these provide insight into how marketing dollars can be spent most efficiently to provide the greatest "bang for the buck." If, for example, Lotus learns that (1) while Microsoft Excel dominates the total non-Lotus market, Borland Quattro Pro accounts for roughly half of the nonloyal non-Lotus market, and (2) nonloyal Quattro customers resemble Lotus loyals more closely than do Lotus nonloyals in terms of what they are looking for in a spreadsheet, then Lotus may conclude that its marketing resources are best allocated to crafting a message convincing Borland customers to try Lotus 1-2-3.[6]

Supply-Side Research

Supply-side research focuses on developing and managing product perceptions. Some of the highest-ROI (return on investment) research is new product research to probe the market for feasibility and demand. By calling prospective customers and telling them about your new product concept, you can find out which features are most important and how customers perceive current product offerings (strengths, weaknesses, opportunities, and threats). More often than not, the results reveal that the competition is too strong, the cost is too high, or additional product work needs to be done. It's much less expensive to make course corrections at this stage than later, when the egos of the product champions take control and politics takes precedence over financial and marketing prudence.

When comprehensively done, supply-side new product research involves identifying the market situation, identifying technology trends and economic/political/social trends, analyzing the competitive environment, measuring market shares, understanding distribution, profiling potential customers, evaluating product features and pricing, identifying the steps customers go through to make initial and ongoing purchase decisions, and making forecasts.

In the next few pages, let's look at the communications audit, the brand audit, message testing, and brand positioning and strategy evaluation.

Communications Audit

A company that has not carefully managed its communications should conduct an audit of all current company and competitive marketing communications to check for consistency and adherence to sound branding principles, find out what brand messages are being repeated and communicated through the current communication materials, and evaluate marketing communications effectiveness.

Brand Audit

Conduct a brand audit to understand what the brand stands for today and what should be changed; identify the criteria, features, and values that are most closely linked to the purchase decision; find out the extent to which these perceptions and associations are positive, negative, owned by the company brand, owned by competitive brands, and generic to the category; assess which attributes are most valued by customers and rank them; and research the benefits, leverage points, consequences, and values behind those key attributes.

Message Testing

Messages are one of the most important factors to test in TechnoBranding. Message testing provides an input and feedback mechanism for the customer from concept through impact. It enables the brand marketer to evaluate brand name alternatives, brand positioning, and strategies; determine strengths and weaknesses; select and rank the best brand associations; determine credibility and uniqueness; and determine brand dominance potential. Most importantly, it enables you to understand what the name or messages actually mean to the customer. This is important because customers almost always take away a meaning different from what the company intended.

Brand Positioning and Strategy Evaluation

Focus groups with current customers, competitors' customers, and selected noncustomers are the easiest and least expensive way to evaluate brand positioning and strategies.

The optimal way to segment customers and target messages is through quantitative surveys. Such a survey begins with identification of your target audiences and customers. Then, a statistically projectable sample is interviewed, usually by telephone. The questionnaire begins by qualifying the prospect (does he or she use the product and is he or she a decision maker?). The goal is to find the people with the power to purchase your product or the power to veto the purchase and to find out which attributes are most important to them when making their purchase decision. A long list of attributes, features, and brand messages, usually developed and culled from a series of focus groups done before the quantitative survey, are read to the person, who is asked to rate how important they are in the purchase decision. It's that simple, although both the formatting and wording of the questionnaire and the interviewing are best left to professionals in order to get reliable data. From the results, cross tabulations can be done to reveal what different target groups are looking for and help sell to them more effectively.

Ongoing Brand Tracking

TechnoBranding is not a one-time fix. It is an ongoing process. Research doesn't stop once the brand has been defined. Studies should be done on a regular basis to track brand awareness, consideration, and loyalty; to find out what's working and what isn't; to track pre- and postmarketing communications effectiveness; to measure and evaluate brand effectiveness; to grow your brand as customers change; and to become more sophisticated. It is especially important to research line and brand extensions to make sure they make sense and will work.

By establishing a model of brand effectiveness, you can identify the signs of change early on and be ready to make appropriate changes and shifts. This chapter gives only a simplified overview of brand research techniques. Advanced quantitative methods, such as choice-based and ratings-based conjoint analysis, can help you conduct "what if" scenarios, quantify the strength and dollar equity in your brand, calculate the exact dollar value of your brand, create models for calculating the effect of price changes on demand, evaluate alternative strategies for increasing market share, and identify the premium price that can be charged for your brand over others.

While research and planning are not substitutes for quality products, they are underutilized tools. It's a rare high-tech company that does too much research and planning. Research is relatively inexpensive, especially when compared to R&D and product development budgets. Research is like TQC (total quality control) before quality became number one in manufacturing. It's available and it's proven. It also offers a highly leveragable competitive advantage to those smart enough to use it.

Notes

1. James R. Tindall, "Marketing Established Brands," *Journal of Consumer Marketing* 8, no. 4 (Fall 1991): 5–11.
2. Edward M. Tauber, "Fit and Leverage in Brand Extensions," in *Brand Equity & Advertising*, ed. David A. Aaker and Alexander L. Biel (Hillsdale, N.J.: Lawrence Erlbaum Associates, 1993), 314–315.
3. Wendy Gordon, "Accessing the Brand through Research," in *Understanding Brands*, ed. Don Cowley (London: Kogan Page Limited, 1991), 39–50.

4. Gian Carlo Bisone, "The Revitalization of the Compaq Brand Name," Brand Tech Forum, Dallas, October 13–14, 1993.
5. International Data Group, "Buying I.T. in the '90s: How to Target," Boston, 1993.
6. International Data Group, "Buying I.T. in the '90s: How to Target," Boston, 1993.

6

Defining the Brand

"There is great power in owning a word (brand association) in the customer's mind. And, don't try to own a brand
association already owned by someone else. To own one
brand association, you have to give up trying to own ten."

Al Reis and Jack Trout[1]

Brand definition starts with (1) a positioning statement, (2) brand
associations, (3) nodal maps, and (4) brand ladders. These four
elements shape the brand's personality, or its creative expression,
through brand names, logos, trademarks, slogans, taglines, characters, and the brand's look and feel.

Brand building is like making friends. We look for people we
like, feel good about, and like being around. We don't choose
friends just because of their physical attributes (well, yes, they do
play a part!). In the "old days," people had personal relationships
with shopkeepers. Nowadays, those one-on-one relationships are
pretty much gone. Replacing that feeling of personal contact and
caring is the challenge of modern brand building.

Think of brands as people, with personalities. Dan Bockman,
Floathe Johnson's creative director, recommends finding a picture
of what your typical customer looks like and then writing a short
monologue of that person talking about the brand. Try this for
your own product. Then, keep it in front of you when you're for-
mulating marketing plans or writing ad copy or developing a concept for a video or commercial. It's a very effective technique for
connecting with your customer.

The objective is to build brands that charm their way into customers' minds and hearts. The most effective way to do this is

inspired brand definition, creatively and consistently expressed in a stand-out package and advertising.

The positioning statement, in one sentence or a short paragraph, answers the question, "What makes you unique and better?" Brand associations are attributes linked to the brand by customers. The goal is to identify the associations that will most influence the purchase of the company's products.

Nodal mapping helps to visually bridge the gap between technical definitions, which technical people need, and customer perceptions, which are ultimately subjective. Both positioning statements and brand associations help combine the power of the mind, or rational self, and the heart, or emotional/cultural self. Brand ladders link features, benefits, and values together into a unified message.

When defining your brand, apply the following criteria. Your brand should:

- Communicate a highly ranked customer need or want.
- Be easily understood and remembered.
- Not be owned already by a competitor.
- Be credible and appealing.

This chapter examines the four tools used in brand definition: the positioning statement, brand associations, nodal maps, and brand ladders.

The Positioning Statement

A positioning statement is a one- or two-sentence statement that clearly and succinctly explains how your product (or company) is different from your competitors'. It is customer- and benefit-oriented. It ensures delivery of a consistent product message and the best product message. It prevents your competition from positioning your product to their advantage.

Positioning is the foundation for strategic brand planning. Its time horizon is usually one to two years in technology markets. It needs to be credible and believable from the beginning and should be updated over time as the product or company evolves.

A positioning statement should:

- Define your prime prospects by their concerns, wants, and needs, as concretely and personally as possible.
- Establish your one point of difference, i.e., the *one* thing that gets people to buy your product instead of the competition's.
- Be your declared "position," your most repeated message to the world.

The most successful positioning strategies persuade through reason and motivate by appealing to personal values and emotions.

There are different levels of positioning and branding: the company, the market, the product line, and the product itself. While ideally it may be best to start with the associations and values that reside at the corporate level (e.g., quality, service) before adding specifics relating to market(s) or product(s), in actual fact, many times the company is born out of the initial successful products.

For example, Apple's corporate positioning has always been based on the original dream of "one person, one computer." Add to that the notion of "the computer for the rest of us." The philosophy behind these statements is the idea that the individual, one person, can change the world and make it a better place. Apple's market positioning has for years been in graphic or creative-based markets, whether in large corporations or small consultancies. The product positioning can almost be summarized by the word *intuitive* by virtue of the user interface and consistency across applications software.

Let's look at how Edmark, a company that creates educational software for the early childhood market (two to ten years old), is developing its position. Sally Narodick, CEO of Edmark, believes that "the importance of brand depends on the company strategy. Our strategy is to develop a very focused niche. We're carving out a small market segment, and we want a very dominant position in it." One key difference between Edmark and its competitors is that Edmark is an educational company using technology as a medium, whereas many of its competitors are technology companies trying to apply their technology in education as well as in other areas.

For the past several years, Edmark has been working on the

relationship between the Edmark corporate brand, its product line brands, and individual product brands. According to Narodick, "retailers and the product reviewers absolutely, firmly believe that they're selling individual product titles." To get the benefits of a corporate brand name as well as product brand names, Edmark is developing families of products and emphasizes company brand associations on its product packaging, on the materials inside the box, and in the fulfillment materials sent to people who return the product registration cards.

You can't communicate well unless you know what you want to say. Positioning is valuable because it serves as a lightning rod to clarify corporate focus and direction, it simplifies the product and company for the customer, and it gives customers a simple way to remember you. It preempts a competitor's attempts to position your company or product for you and gives you a device against which to measure the success of your brand communications programs.

How Is the Positioning Statement Developed?

Research is used during the positioning development process to make sure the statement fits and works with customers' existing attitudes. Avoid feature-based positioning factors. Look for intangible positioning factors; they'll last longer and be more effective. The positioning statement should be as specific as possible as to the target market (e.g., job titles, income level, interests). Avoid the tendency to be general and to be all things to all people. Instead of approaching it on a conceptual level, get specific and down to earth. Speak in the vernacular. Use the words that customers use when they speak of your company and what you do for them. Then test, experiment, try it out, and change when needed.

The positioning statement is based on the perceptions of both your management team and the marketplace. The basis for positioning is qualitative research on each member of the management team, key employees, large shareholders, selected industry editors and analysts/gurus, customers, key user sites or luminaries, dealers/distributors, and prospects. Preferably, quantitative research on customers is included.

Once this information is compiled, a preliminary positioning statement is created based on how these groups differentiate the product. Because it's based on the marketplace, positioning will need to be revisited at least once a year or whenever there are major shifts or developments in the marketplace.

Here are some questions to think about when writing a positioning statement. In general, the more specific your answers can be, the better.

- What is the target market?
- Who is the user or buyer?
- What is the product category?
- In the simplest terms possible, what are your customers buying from you and how would you describe your business?
- What is the most important reason that people buy your product?
- What makes you better than your competitors?

After your first draft, reread your positioning statement and ask yourself, "If a room of buyers was shown this statement, would they be able to identify it as ours?"

Once created and written, the "strawman" positioning statement is presented to management, ideally in a session mediated by an outside facilitator. The facilitator elicits responses to the statement and gradually adapts it through management consensus. Typically, the final statement is completely different from the initial statement but still supports the research conclusions.

The interactive positioning session needs some ground rules—for example, everyone participates, no one dominates, no ideas are trounced, and no one leaves until agreement is reached. Appoint one person to take the role of a critical customer to make sure the statement truly differentiates, doesn't use jargon, and is customer-oriented rather than vendor-oriented. Appoint one person to take the role of a critical employee to make sure the statement will work internally.

Positioning Statement Considerations

First, define what it is not. A positioning statement *is not* a tagline, a slogan, or a mission statement.

In general, mission statements are a waste of time and represent only the inside view of top management. You certainly can't expect employees to have two statements of company vision or purpose on their walls. It's hard enough to remember and relate to one. Mission statements are the company talking to itself. It is far better to concentrate on developing a positioning statement based on both the inside view and the customers' perceptions of the company that will help employees understand what your customers really care about.

Mission statements come from the head, vision statements come from the heart, and positioning statements come from both the head and the heart. Mission statements are about company or "me" thinking. Positioning statements are about others—in particular, about customers' acceptance. This buy-in and playback by the market is the definition of success in positioning.

The positioning statement may include the product's position in relation to other products in the market. This is particularly effective if there is an added virtue to that position, such as being the market leader, the highest/lowest-cost producer, number two, or even smallest. Also, positioning must speak to the customer and the channel. At the same time, it must project the corporate culture, be deeply ingrained in the customer's perception of the products, and help lead the company into the future.

"A TechnoBranding workshop helped me to understand everything that a positioning statement needs to contain," says Mark Craemer, product manager, marketing, PageAhead Software Corporation. "What was missing from ours was the distinguishing factor that sets our company's product apart from others." TechnoBranding can make your product stand out in the eyes of the consumer, and that's important because consumers go with what they know.

Don't do a positioning statement like this meaningless one:

"General Widgets is a leading supplier of advanced, high-performance, quality products for sophisticated companies with a commitment to power, ease-of-use, and increased productivity." This positioning statement is filled with abstract and overused words like *advanced* and *quality.* Rather than "sophisticated companies," say something like "service companies with 25 to 250 employees." Be as specific as you can. Every company struggles with its unique points of difference. In this situation, less is more. The fewer the points of difference, the easier it will be to establish your position.

Here are some sample positioning statements for you to study.

Omega Environmental Corporate Position Statement

Omega Environmental, Inc. provides UST [underground storage tank] and AST [above-ground storage tank] owners throughout North America with turnkey regulatory compliance through its extensive construction network, equipment sales and service, engineering experience, remediation services, leak prevention technology, and related insurance and financial programs. The Omega team reduces risk and delivers cost-effective regulatory compliance, today and into the future.

Omega Environmental, Inc. is a Bothell, Washington–based company that provides advanced products and services for environmentally safe storage of liquids, and for cleanup of contaminated soils throughout North America.

Omega is the first company in the petroleum business to establish a national network of affiliates. "We know that this is one of the most important benefits we offer our customers, and the positioning statement helped us clarify how the rest of our services fit within that picture," says Maurice Schafer, vice president of marketing and sales at Omega. "It provides a format for us to look at our services from the customer's point of view, and come to agreement internally on what is most important."

Panlabs Positioning Statement

Panlabs has mastered the art of identifying therapeutic leads and developing and improving products and processes. With interdisciplinary teams functioning as a client's strategic research partner, Panlabs gives pharmaceutical companies affordable innovation on novel projects and rapid, reliable solutions to routine projects.

"I think it's important in the generic marketplace today to build an identity for the manufacturer's name," says Floyd Willison, vice president, sales and marketing, Panlabs. "The brand name of the product isn't going to help you as much as it used to."

Panlabs is a service company, selling biotechnology services to pharmaceutical companies. Willison believes that it's the brand identification of the company itself that separates Panlabs' service from someone else's. "While we have some trademarked names in our service line, the brand name most important to us is the company identification itself," Willison says.

Differentiating a service business, and especially a generic service business, is a challenge for many companies. The key is to carefully position the company, not only for customers or clients, but so employees can all know how the company is separating itself from the competition. According to Willison, what the positioning process did for Panlabs was to bring about a broad consensus within the company as to what Panlabs' primary service opportunities are, while providing a focus for the company in terms of defining its product and bringing a strategic approach to the company's marketing efforts.

Now It's Your Turn

Fill in the blanks in this sentence for your own quick positioning statement:

"For people who [describe the target users], [insert your company or brand name] is the company/brand of [describe your competitive set] that provides [tell the benefit that makes you different and better]."

Here's a made-up example:

"For people who are male, seven to sixteen years old, and living in middle-class neighborhoods, Radway is the brand of skateboards that maximizes maneuverability."

The target users are those desired customers who share common needs or demographic/psychographic characteristics. The competitive set may be as simple as a product category, but should always be worded in the way that customers describe the category. The benefit that makes you better is the one point of difference you want most closely associated with the product or company brand. One benefit has much more power than two and will avoid the likelihood that customers will get confused.

The "3B" positioning test will help you to quickly determine if a positioning statement is on target. Standing alone, does the statement allow the audience to understand your:

- Philosophy of Business
- Product Benefits
- What makes you Better?

To make your positioning statement even more down-to-earth and credible, add on a sentence that says:

"Unlike [insert your main competitor], [insert your company or brand name] [tell the one benefit that makes you different from the competitor]."

Geoffrey Moore on Positioning

We live in a relative world. Positioning requires something to position against. Position can be expressed, or mapped in a visual format, on an X/Y graph, as explained by Geoffrey Moore, author of *Crossing the Chasm*.[2] As illustrated in Figure 6-1, the X axis is the key benefit that buyers, either consciously or unconsciously, want from the purchase. This could be just about anything: a feature (e.g., reliability), a benefit (e.g., ease of use), a culturally based factor (e.g., prestige, status), or a specific need (e.g., a car for a family with three or more children). This is the way customers sort their buying choices. For example, if a person is buying a car that needs to be good in snow, that eliminates a Miata, but includes a four-wheel drive car. The further to the right of the X axis the product scores, the better.

The X-axis benefit reduces your choices and the Y axis is the final sorting factor that you use to decide among the remaining choices. For example, sticking with the illustration of cars, if you want one that drives well in snow, you might be selecting from a

Figure 6-1. Using an *X/Y* graph to create a positioning map and get away from the market leader.

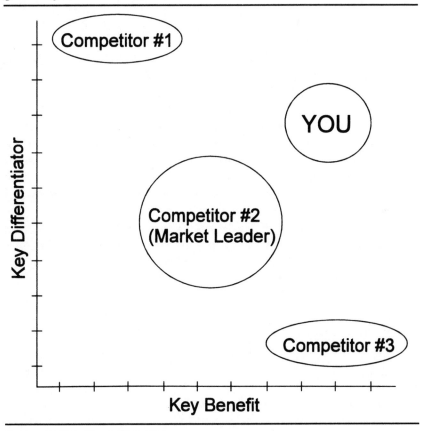

Source: Geoffrey Moore Consulting.

Range Rover, a Toyota, and a Jeep. If you pick the Range Rover, it would probably mean you want status; if you pick the Toyota, a lot of people would say you want quality; if you picked the Jeep, it would probably mean you want to buy American.

Moore explains that two variables are about all a large marketplace can sustain. It's not that people don't have three or more variables in their buying decisions, but that large markets won't form around those types of products because it's too complicated; people can't explain it, they can't rationalize it, they can't say it to each other quickly enough—it's just too hard. Note: This technique for mapping perceptions and the buying process works well with almost all products. Try it!

The fundamental rule of positioning is, always work with two variables. "Your goal is to name the axes; if you can name the axes, you can win the game," Moore says. This is a good way to segment markets. Look for people who want the two same buying factors— for example, people who have three or more children and who want a four-wheel-drive vehicle.

How do you enter a market that has a dominant market leader? If you can't be number one or two in a category, invent a new category. Using the X/Y axis, the object is to get a position high and to the right. As illustrated in Figure 6-1, put a numeral "1" high up and next to the Y axis, put a numeral "2" in the middle of the space, and next to the X axis, but way out to the right, put a numeral "3."

By definition, market leaders tend to take a lot of the space in their marketplace. For example, if you say "laser printers," it must be Hewlett-Packard; if you say "operating systems," it must be Microsoft. No matter what you label the X or Y axis, the market leader will probably be at the "2" position, and it will soak up a lot of the market. Even in those areas in which it isn't a specialist, it will have some of the business.

"In any market you enter where you position against a market leader, you will lose," Moore says. "The reason is, and this is particularly true if there's some anxiety about what to buy, people will always tend to buy the market leader."

Therefore, differentiating against a market leader never works because the market won't give you "permission" to do that. The market leader owns the large central space. Rather, try to differentiate against competitor "3." Identify a feature, benefit, or need where you can clearly excel the market leader. In order to communicate that superiority to the marketplace, instead of saying, "I am better than '2'" (the market leader), what you say is, "I am as good as, if not better than, competitor '3' but I am also different from '3,'" according to Moore. This second, differentiating factor is whatever you have determined to put on the Y axis.

"For example, when Convex entered the market with a very good minicomputer, if they had positioned against the DEC VAX, they would have lost because DEC VAX was a market leader," says

Moore. Instead, since Convex had a mathematically fast minicomputer, it positioned against Cray supercomputer.

As Moore explains it, on the X/Y axis, Convex put Cray in position "3," DEC in position "2," and the Sun Microsystems workstation in position "1." The X axis was called "supercomputing calculations," and the Y axis was "price."

Rather than saying, "We're a better VAX," Convex said, "We're a cheaper Cray." So instead of calling its product a "super minicomputer," which it wanted to do originally but which would have positioned it against DEC, it called the product a "mini-supercomputer" and positioned it against Cray.

The reason this works is if Convex had positioned its product as a super minicomputer against DEC, DEC would have had to retaliate because if it did not, it would have been agreeing that Convex's product was better than VAX.

However, Convex was agreeing with Cray's statement, which was, "We're the best supercomputer in the world." Convex said, "If you can't afford a Cray, you can get about one-quarter of a Cray for about one-tenth of the price," which is where the Convex price was. Cray said, "We're not going to discount, and we don't make a small Cray, so if you can't afford a regular-size Cray, you might as well get a Convex."

DEC said, "We are the leading minicomputer vendor in this industry," and Convex said, "That's correct. We are not a minicomputer, we are a mini-supercomputer; we're in a niche." DEC said, "We're not in that niche," so DEC left Convex alone.

Sun said, "We are the best low-cost engineering workstation in the market," and Convex agreed. Convex said, "We are specializing in high-end calculations," and Sun said, "We don't do that."

So, Convex was left alone, and most importantly, it was left alone by the market leader. Convex ended up taking market share from DEC, and some from Cray. It didn't set off DEC's defense mechanism because it said, "We're just going to take this little niche."

"You don't position directly against a market leader; you bounce your positioning off a niche leader and differentiate yourself from them," Moore says. By doing this, you end up creating a new space, which is high and to the right of the X/Y axis.

The goal is to create a new space in the market for yourself.

Describe a position that gets you outside the gravitational field of the market leader, where you can define a brand identity of your own. That gets you a foothold. Then you can work to increase the size of your position. If you've looked ahead to where the majority of customers are going in their purchases, and included that information in your positioning definition, you are in the best position to grab market share and, if you have a little luck, perhaps become the new leader.

Brand Associations

Broadly defined, brand associations are what your publics know about your brand and how they feel about buying it. Associations are more than company/product features, benefits, or attributes. They are the essence of how we order what we know about a company or product. That order, which is a rational/emotional construct, can be changed. It can be enhanced or diminished, and the order of importance of that knowledge can be altered, to the extent that people who would never consider themselves prospects could turn into clients.

We call these constructs *associations*. The association concept closely matches with how our brains file and remember information. By identifying and mapping our associations, we can begin to actively and purposefully communicate them to prospects. Our final goal is to have the agreed-upon company/product associations reflected in the minds of our prospects.

One method for uncovering your brand associations is to put them into a different context by creating a metaphor (literally *changed form*). One popular brand/metaphor exercise is to define the company's personality as if it were a person. (Ask the question, "If my company was a character or a famous person, who would it be?") Another is to ask what kind of an animal or what brand of car the company would be. Another good one is to ask, "If the brand died tomorrow, what would be on its tombstone?"

Because brand identity is largely stored as sensory impressions, imagine that you're walking down a street with each house's front door marked with a brand name. What will you see, feel, smell, hear, taste when you open your home's door?

Two things to keep in mind: People identify with other people and with animals. Their images are appealing and memorable. It's not just Jell-O that people remember, it's Bill Cosby. Many people in the computer industry still remember the HP Dalmatians even though it's been several years since they appeared. In packaged goods, can you identify what product goes with Mr. Whipple, Aunt Jemima, Dutch Boy, Betty Crocker, and the Jolly Green Giant? In many cases, the character and the brand have become one. In high-tech, Peter Norton, Bill Gates, and Charlie Chaplin are also easy for us to remember and associate with their company brands. Certainly, people and animal images are easier to remember than taglines and slogans.

An association might be a product attribute, benefit, person, animal, logo or graphic device, product or company category, competitor, the company's standing or reputation, price/performance/value, or even the customer's lifestyle.

Concrete and Abstract Associations

There are two types of associations: concrete and abstract. Concrete associations are benefit- and feature-oriented and are the most typical associations currently being used in the high-tech world. They are usually being used by default, i.e., a company hasn't identified them as its associations, but sees them as benefits or features. Therefore, they are not continued over the long term. Further, no attention is given to how defendable the associations are. They can typically be eroded by changes in competitive technology. However, an industry leader, such as HP, often has concrete associations that are defendable. In HP's case, the longest MTBF (mean time before failure) or reliability may be a defendable product association.

Abstract associations are intangible (emotional) and usually related to images customers regard as positive or pleasing. These are symbols such as Apple's Apple or IBM's Charlie Chaplin and Pink Panther; and slogans, logos, and attitudes (such as clever, smart, and helpful) that act as memory shorthand for the company or product. Market leaders that introduce and sustain abstract associations over a five- to ten-year period will have a significant advantage over their competitors. And, according to a study by leading consumer brand-building agency Leo Burnett, "brands with greater equity have stronger, more intense and more focused emotional associations."[3]

It's one thing to measure tangible features and attributes of brands. It's more difficult to get a handle on the intangibles, those abstract feelings and images that customers have in their minds about the brand. Sal Randazzo, senior vice president/director of strategic planning at DMB&B, New York, uses a "nifty little research tool" he calls the Brand Identity Profile (BIP).[4]

In focus groups, he asks consumers to list all their associations with the brand. Then, qualitatively or quantitatively, consumers are asked to rank the degree to which each element connotes the brand name. The end result is a prioritized list of the attributes, emotions, benefits, and things that are most strongly associated with the brand—a BIP. The BIP is then compared to competitive brand BIPs. Finally, the elements at the top of the list are qualitatively probed to get a better understanding of what these elements mean in the consumer's mind.

Identifying Associations

Defining brand associations is best done by an outside, objective consultant or an agency in partnership with the chief marketing executive and the management team. Preliminary associations are created and worked out through a series of consultant/agency-mediated sessions with management. It is assumed that research that shows how the company or product is currently perceived by the company and the market infrastructure has already been done.

If quantitative research has been done to statistically identify and rank attribute options for brand associations, the concrete brand associations should be self-selecting. Abstract associations related to the brand personality will probably come from the advertising agency as part of the creative process. If quantitative research has not been done, focus groups should be used to determine how well those associations match customers' perceptions.

As with positioning, associations need to be reviewed annually to determine progress and to consider adding associations.

How to Use Positioning Statements and Associations

The positioning statement and brand associations are not intended to be quoted word for word; rather, they are to be used as the source or guide for all messages. To solidly build brand identity and brand equity, embed the positioning statement and brand associations intelligently in all communications: advertising, public relations, literature, direct mail, trade shows, packaging, dealer materials, seminars, and employee communications.

Employees should have both the positioning statement and the associations posted in a visible spot near their telephones so that they can refer to them when communicating with any of the company's publics, including prospects, customers, and suppliers. The idea is for employees to translate those values into their own words. This ensures that all members of the team give a consistent message, one that is most likely to contain purchase-influencing differentiators.

Nodal Maps

Another method for defining brand associations is the network activation theory. It states that brand information is stored in your memory in "nodes," or concepts. Each node can store very different things, like describers of the category or product, company names, love, things that are fast, etc. The most important nodes are those tied to the purchase decision.

The mind also builds prototypes for these concepts or secondary associations that are connected to the original concept. For example, when you think of fast, you might think of your favorite fast car. Once these node associations are set, they become automatic, and a person thinks or concentrates on finer points or other subjects. Therefore, if you want someone to grasp a message or concept, make it as familiar as possible.

For example, leverage cultural or socially relevant concepts, such as fashion and what's perceived as hip, cool, or rad by the target audience. (Perfume ads are good at this.) Knowing the nodes of your product and your competition's products will give you a basis for changing them into what you want them to be.

To get started, use research to find out what node associations are stored in customers' memory and how they are organized in order to make the brand easy to remember. Through experience with the brand, our minds network nodes together into idea families. When one node is stimulated, the entire network is activated, resulting in feelings of familiarity, quality, and rightness. Like muscles, when nodes are exercised (through advertising and public relations), they become stronger. Through the power of creative persuasion, you can literally get inside people's minds and hearts and change perceptions.

The value of mapping associations and creating nodal maps is that they give a mental picture of the brand that can be used to bring consistency to all forms of marketing communications, regardless of the media used. This is also a good way to reverse-engineer a competitor's messages. For example, Figure 6-2 shows one version of a nodal map for Microsoft. Another nodal map is found in Figure 4-2.

An Exercise in Nodal Mapping

Start with your product or company name in the middle of a piece of paper and draw a circle around it. Think of your customers. What do they look like? What kinds of things do they say when talking about the use of your product? Then, imagine you are asking them the question, "If you could list only three reasons why you buy our product rather than one from another company, what would they be?" The answers you hear are the brand associations, the messages, that you want to communicate to all current and prospective customers. Keep the associations simple and limited to one or two words in length, if possible. Then, apply the following criteria for brand association selection:

- Valued by customer
- Believable, sustainable, and appropriate
- Able to create positive feelings and make people feel good about the brand
- Defendable
- Fits market's perception of brand

Figure 6-2. Hypothetical Microsoft nodal map.

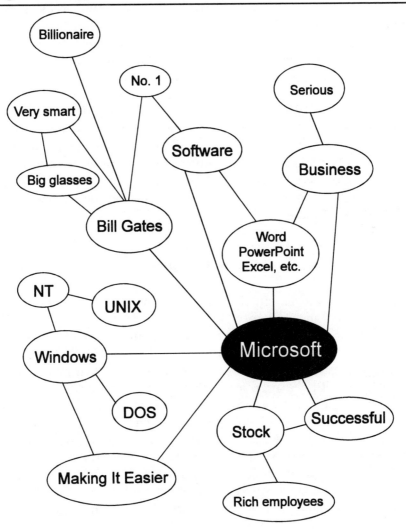

- Naturally connected to brand
- Different from competitors
- Proven by research to be tied to purchase
- Easy to remember

The brand associations that are left are those you attach to your brand name by drawing spokes out from your center circle, writing the brand association, and drawing a circle around it to create a node. Ideally, you've come to your brand associations through research with customers. You *know* why they buy and remain loyal. By including these brand associations in all your marketing communications, you provide the stimulus that helps them to buy again and again.

After you have created your basic nodal map, you can add secondary associations to each of the two or three brand associations. To get secondary associations, find out what customers think when they think of the primary brand association. For example, if your brand association is "reliable," the secondary associations might be "doesn't break down" or "I can count on it." Look at Figures 6-2, 6-5, and 6-7 to see how nodes can be mapped and relate to one another.

Brand Ladders

Brand ladders are a method of modeling the mental and emotional process customers follow when making product purchase decisions. The theory is that the more emotionally attached customers are to the brand, the more likely they will be to buy it and recommend it. It is a directional model, starting with features usually associated with the product itself. It gradually moves from the product to the person and what the product means and does for him or her as a human being, emotionally and culturally.

As illustrated in Figure 6-3, a brand ladder starts with a product's most important attribute or feature (e.g., fast) and links it to its benefit (e.g., no waiting or wasted time), the resulting job value (e.g., get more done, be more productive), and the emotional value to the individual (e.g., feel good about what is accomplished, self-actualization).

The first step in building a brand ladder is to identify which attributes are important to customers when they are considering a product purchase. Attributes are performance-related features, such as reliable, fast, NetWare-compatible, and Windows-compatible, that customers associate with the product and include in the selection process.

Once you identify the key attributes, ask customers (through

Figure 6-3. Brand ladder example.

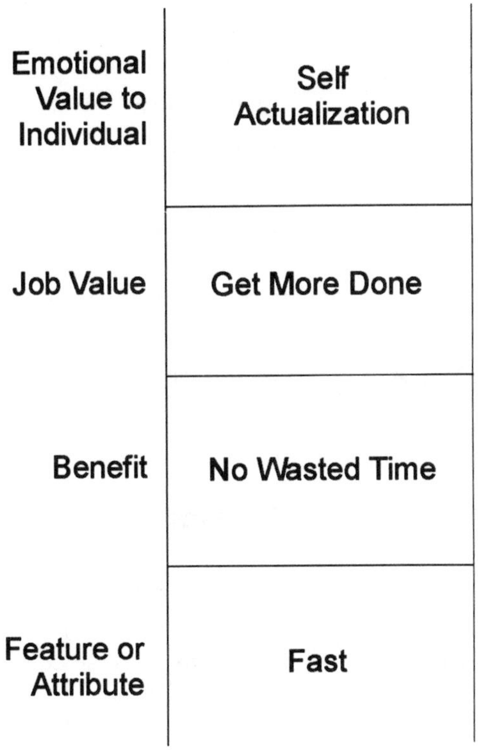

Emotional Value to Individual	Self Actualization
Job Value	Get More Done
Benefit	No Wasted Time
Feature or Attribute	Fast

one-on-one interviews, focus groups, and surveys) which attribute was most important to them in their product selection. Then ask, "Why is that attribute important to you?" and "What is the benefit of that attribute in your work (or personal) situation?" As the number of interviews increases, multiple benefits will become clear. Examples are: helps me be more productive, helps me meet deadlines, and makes my job easier. After each answer, keep asking, "Why is that important to you?" and see how far up the ladder you can go. Then you will be able to map "heavily traveled" paths (ones that the brand owns). Through the use of the same kind of research on competitive brands, brand managers can identify the messages that can be "purchased" with minimal investment.

Don't be constrained by the structure of attribute–benefit–job value–emotional value. It's only a guide to understand what the

Figure 6-4. Hypothetical brand ladder based on reliability.

Emotional Value	Self Actualization
Job Value	Do a Better Job
Job Value	Efficiency
Benefit	No Breakdowns
Feature	Reliability

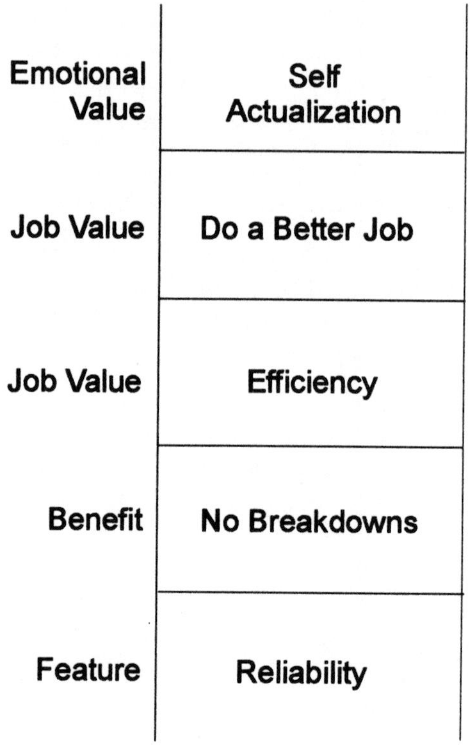

brand's attributes mean to people in their work and personal life.

Not all products affect customers' emotional values. It takes time and a strong brand relationship to reach the point where a brand elicits feelings of self-esteem, accomplishment, or self-actualization.

Of all high-tech products, reliability is the attribute customers rank most highly. Figure 6-4 shows a hypothetical brand ladder based on reliability, which might apply to anything from a computer to an appliance. Reliability means no hassles in how the product operates (no breakdowns), saving time and money, eliminating maintenance frustration, creating happy users, and doing what it's supposed to. For the user, the benefits of a reliable product are efficiency, productivity, no wasted time, and things getting done. In addition, the users feel they've made the right decision and don't feel open to criticism. That means that users don't associate stress with the product and feel more comfortable about their job or task, enabling them to feel like they're doing a better job. The values that these might bring to the individual are self-actualization, self-esteem, satisfaction in a job well done, and job security.

Brand ladders go beyond product features and attributes to identify the significant and personal relevance attached to these attributes. To put it in the vernacular, they identify what's cool and what turns customers on. They use the customer's own words and phrases, and they reveal how features, benefits, and related personal values influence and stimulate sales.

Brand Ladders and Nodal Maps in the Marine Market

Heart Interface is a small but rapidly growing high-tech company that manufactures inverters and battery chargers that provide silent AC power for boats and RVs. "Picking a brand name is important," says Warren Stokes, senior vice president and general manager. "Heart is a good name. I like it because it has the same sort of appeal that Apple has; it's easy to remember, and it has a positive image associated with it." Heart's most recent series of inverters is called the Freedom series, which is a well-known brand within its markets.

As part of a TechnoBrand consulting project, sailboat and powerboat customers were interviewed to determine the reasons Heart Interface inverter/chargers were purchased and to measure customer satisfaction in a number of areas. Since Heart asks on its warranty cards for customers to indicate purchase factors, we already knew that silent AC power, high efficiency, and company reputation were the three most important purchase factors. In the survey, we asked boat owners which one of those factors was most important. Then we read a list of benefits for each factor and asked boat owners what the benefit meant to them. Information collected from the survey was the basis for the nodal map and brand ladder shown in Figures 6-5 and 6-6.

The surveys provided more detail and understanding of what the purchase factors actually meant to customers. This resulted in a rewording of the three main brand factors associated with Heart

Figure 6-5. Heart Interface brand association nodal map for marine markets.

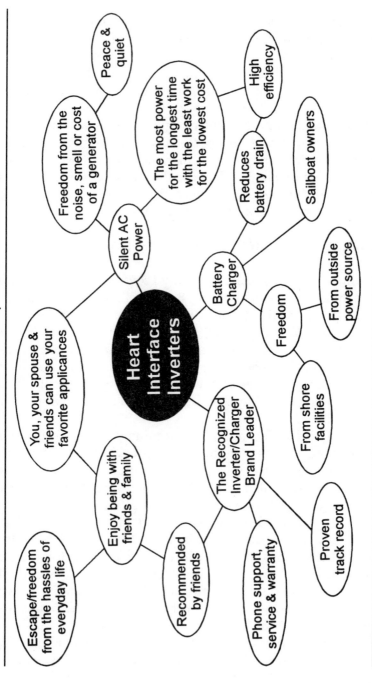

Source: Heart Interface, created by Floathe Johnson.

Figure 6-6. Heart Interface brand ladder for marine markets.

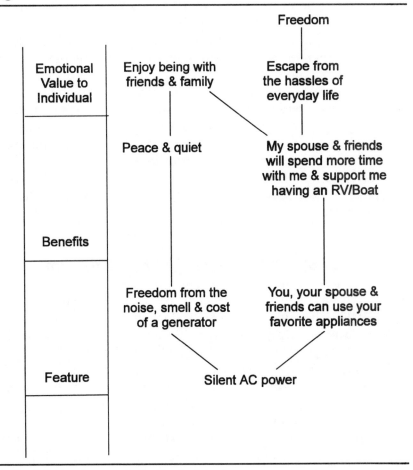

Source: Heart Interface, created by Floathe Johnson.

Interface inverters: silent AC power, battery charger, and the recognized inverter/charger brand leader. Silent AC power has secondary associations of freedom from the noise of a generator, the ability of a spouse to use favorite appliances (the highest-rated attribute), and the most power for the least cost. Battery charging is linked with reducing battery drain, increasing efficiency, and bringing freedom from shore facilities and outside power sources. The recognized brand leader is supported by the high level of word-of-mouth advertising prevalent in the boating community, the excellent phone support provided by Heart, and its proven track record over the years.

Here's what a typical customer might think about Heart inverter/chargers: "Heart inverters and chargers enable me, my wife, and friends to use their favorite appliances, making my boat more attractive to them. At the same time, the inverter/charger frees me from outside power sources and the noise of a generator. What this boils down to is that I can escape from the hassles of everyday life, spend more time on my boat, and enjoy the free-dom of being out on the water, away from it all." Can you see how this perception of Heart products can be used to more effectively communicate not only to customers' minds, but to their hearts as well?

The Applied Microsystems Frog Campaign

Defining positioning statements and brand associations is not an end in itself. They are researched and created in order to be used over and over in advertising and public relations so that eventually customers will automatically associate the desired words, images, and feelings with the brand name. To show you how it works in real life, let's take a look at how positioning and brand associations are actually being used in an advertising campaign.

Brand is as important in niche markets as it is in mass mar-kets. Applied Microsystems manufactures tools that help engi-neers design and debug the computer chips found in everything from laser printers to cellular phones. "Brand is very important and something that you associate with larger, more mature compa-nies," says Steve Dearden, vice president of Applied Microsystems. "The importance of the HP brand name in high-technology mar-kets is a good example. People assume all kinds of things about HP that may, in fact, not be true."

The TechnoBranding process is valuable with complex, tech-nical products because the types of people that you're dealing with in high-tech companies, mostly engineers, primarily don't think about the human element. They're very analytical. While the engineers within Applied Microsystems were a little bit skeptical at the beginning of the process, they've seen the results.

None of Applied Microsystems' competitors have built a strong brand identity. "We want to be one of the first in our category to establish brand identity," states Teri Wiegman, director of marketing communications at Applied Microsystems at the time this campaign was created. "Our business is very competitive, and all the competitors look the same, with the same features and the same price. The branding efforts have helped us rise above that."

Here is Applied Microsystems' positioning statement:

> The embedded systems expert and innovation leader, Applied Microsystems helps engineers develop products faster, more reliably, and with a lower cost per seat through a combination of affordable CodeTAP emulators, full-scale emulators, and a growing family of other compatible design and debug tools.

Figure 6-7 shows the actual brand association nodal map for Applied Microsystems. One of the brand associations identified to communicate Applied Microsystems' position is a key part of the brand personality: the frog. Frogs are quick, approachable, and "have an attitude," which are attributes valued by the target audiences: engineers and programmers. Not only are frogs nature's best and fastest debugger (the number 1 need among engineers for Applied Microsystems products), they can be shown in groups to represent Applied Microsystems' range of debugging solutions.

Frog ads, like the one shown in Figure 6-8, stand out in trade publications, where most ads show only chips and boards. Each product family has its own frog character, informally called names like Rocket Frog or "Rambo" Frog. Applied Microsystems posters (and ads) are hung in hundreds of engineers' cubicles, sometimes with names for each frog representing various engineers within the company. Within the company and at trade shows, the frog images appear on T-shirts, sweatshirts, buttons, and posters. The frog image has legs! The upshot is that over time, engineers are

(*text continues on page 134*)

Figure 6-7. Applied Microsystems brand association nodal map.

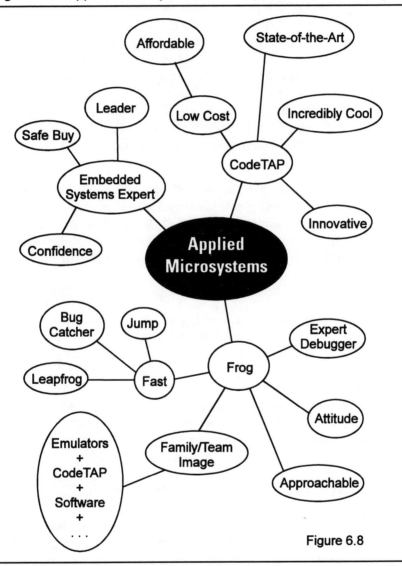

Figure 6.8

Figure 6-8. Applied Microsystems "Rambo" frog ad.

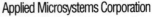
Source: Applied Microsystems, created by Floathe Johnson.

coming to associate fast debugging with the frog and with Applied Microsystems.

"Fast debugging" is an association with real meat and relevancy to it. If you try to build a brand around something that doesn't fit the customer's image of you, you will either fail or spend a lot of money trying.

Some people think frogs and characters are gimmick graphics. Dearden disagrees. "The frog is the most valuable thing to come out of the TechnoBranding process. It's become a sort of company subculture within Applied Microsystems. We're a new company; we've got a different feeling and attitude developing inside the management team and also in the rest of the company. The frog is something that people are able to identify with, which is very positive for the company internally. Customer reaction has generally been very positive. They like it."

The objectives of the program were to generate qualified leads for Applied Microsystems' products and build brand equity by positioning Applied Microsystems as the brand of choice in fulfilling design teams' evolving needs. The quality of sales leads increased significantly, to the point where qualified leads are averaging 40 percent of all inquiries, increasing the effectiveness of the sales force. "The number of leads per ad is consistent, so we can turn the number of leads up or down, as needed," Wiegman says.

Customers and semiconductor companies see a new attitude and new thinking at Applied Microsystems versus the stodgy image that they may have associated with the company. "They're seeing a change in the company and are associating the frog with the change," concludes Dearden.

Notes

1. Al Reis and Jack Trout, *The 22 Immutable Laws of Marketing: Violate Them at Your Own Risk!* (New York: HarperBusiness, 1993).
2. Geoffrey Moore, *Crossing the Chasm: Marketing and Selling Technology Products to Mainstream Customers* (New York: Harper-Business, 1991).

3. Josh McQueen, executive vice president, director of research at the Leo Burnett Company, "Brand Equity and Imagery," *Advertising Research Foundation Executive Research Digest*, Feb. 28, 1991, 1–2.
4. Sal Randazzo, "Build a BIP to Understand Brand's Image," *Marketing News*, Sept. 16, 1991, 18.

7

Integrating Brand Strategy And Marketing Communications

"A brand relationship should be a marriage, not a one-night stand."

Larry Light, Chairman of the Coalition for Brand Equity

With a solid base of research and a customer-oriented brand definition in hand, your next step is to develop plans and strategies to grow the brand through marketing and communications programs.

With the proliferation of new media, more TV channels, and more of everything competing for our time, it's critical that the brand name be simple and easy to remember. Focus on only one or two key messages or associations. Make it easy for the customer to experience the brand through product trial, and encourage the customer to imagine how it feels to use the product. Write copy that directly relates to how the customer evaluates the brand when making the purchase decision. Finally, activate these purchase-stimulating nodes at the point of purchase through packaging, point-of-purchase (POP) displays, offers, contests, and other relationship-building activities.

Always remember the three Cs of brand communications:

1. Consistency
2. Consistency
3. Consistency

Be consistent in how you present your brand to customers. Being concise, making an impact, and being compassionate also help.

Companies like HP, Intel, and Microsoft have a design layout standard for ads and marketing literature. The use of a consistent layout and type style makes it easy for customers to visually identify with your company. A consistent design look is the most cost-effective way to "buy" your company an image of professionalism, reliability, and trustworthiness.

Building brand is more than imposing a design grid on advertisements for different products to achieve a common look and feel. To manage the brand as an asset, transmit the brand vision by developing and using a brand identity handbook. A corporate roadmap for future brand development, the handbook defines corporate communications standards, controls the use of logos and trademarks, gives examples of proper usage, and presents the company's positioning statement(s) and brand associations, as well as the basic nodal maps and brand ladders. This will let everyone in the company know what the company brands stand for and how to communicate the brand correctly, clearly, and consistently in all communications with customers, suppliers, investors, etc.

Integrate brand into all aspects of the company that touch the customer through the four P's of marketing: product, price, promotion, and place. Here are a few examples of how brand can be incorporated into each "P":

- Product—Don't compromise product quality. Remember, it's not the facts that count, it's the perceptions. Given the choice of being first or being better, be first, unless your strength is manufacturing and distribution. First means first in the mind, and owning the category. If you can't be in the top two or three, set up a new category or subdivide one that already exists. Make sure product extensions don't jeopardize the brand equity of the brand name.

- Price—Price should be based on the overall value to the customer.

- Place—Make sure the product is easy to find and in stock, and if it's a global brand, make it available simultaneously, worldwide.

- Promotion—Build brand equity in every marketing communications program or project.

The goal is to make sure that every time the brand is taken down from the shelf, it goes back up with the same amount of equity—or more.

Once a brand identity has been defined and a strong, extendible campaign theme has emerged, how long should the campaign run? How much repetition is enough? The answer comes from ongoing brand awareness tracking studies. Take the Maytag repairman campaign, for instance. The campaign has been running for twenty-six years, making Mr. Lonely the longest-running real-life character on U.S. TV. "We track awareness levels and his (the repairman's) have never been higher," says Norman Boyle, Maytag's director of advertising.[1] Thus, a strong campaign can and should go on and on. Don't be talked into changing a campaign that is working. Practice my "hot button" philosophy, which says, "When you find a hot button that works, sit on it."

Always look for new and customer-relevant places to put the brand name on and in products. Ed Artzt, P&G CEO, is credited with putting the Charmin name on the cardboard tube inside each roll of toilet tissue.[2] What a perfect time to remind customers about the brand. Is there a place you could put your brand name that is equally relevant?

One basic point to keep in mind: Don't conceal your name in advertisements. Include the brand name in headlines.

The objective of advertising and marketing communication is to move the product off the store or warehouse shelf by reinforcing the brand identity and image, again and again. The Duracell bunny ads and the Maytag repairman campaign are excellent examples of advertising programs building brand with the same message, yet still keeping the creative fresh and appealing. Most well-known U.K. ad campaigns, including Mr. Kipling's cakes, Kit-Kat, Andrex, and Hamlet, are over thirty years old.

Integrated Marketing Communications

Neither a "silver bullet" nor a "cure," integrated marketing communications offers companies a powerful but challenging strategy for building strong brand relationships with customers. Customers are bombarded with thousands of messages a day. In the confusion, they look for safety through brand relationships they can trust. Integrated marketing communications (IMC) is like a lighthouse beacon. All of a company's messages on its brand's behalf together become a clear, bright light to guide customers toward the company's products.

Integrated marketing creates the optimal mix of marketing and communications strategies and tactics that will cost-effectively achieve the objectives. Elements that need to be integrated include market research, planning, and analysis; brand definition; advertising, public relations, and direct marketing; inquiry handling and database management; packaging, collateral, trade shows, and channel promotion; in-box promotion; aftermarketing; and product support and services.

How do the experts define IMC? Dave Sutherland, manager of integrated marketing for IBM, speaking at an American Marketing Association luncheon in Seattle about how IBM integrates marketing communications, defined IMC as "a strategic sequence of planned communication events through the best media." The book *Integrated Marketing Communications* by Schultz, Tannenbaum, and Lauterborn describes IMC as "a synchronized multi-channel communications strategy that reaches every market segment with a single unified message." And David Ogilvy defines it simply as "one-stop shopping."[3]

IMC is a strategic cross-disciplinary orchestration of marketing and communications activities, creatively delivering consistent brand messages that persuade customers to buy from and remain loyal to the company's brands.

Building awareness and interest in a new product and reinforcing a purchase are functions of the number and quality of impressions made in a customer's mind. The more times you repeat your message in a variety of media, the more chance you have of getting considered, getting purchased, and then keeping that hard-won customer.

Another aspect of integration is to make sure customers receive messages simultaneously, in all media. If each message is a flashlight, the chances of being seen will be much greater if all flashlights turn toward the customer and turn on at the same time. That's why it's desirable for customers to learn about new products *at the same time* from salespeople, print ads, broadcast ads, direct mail, public relations, point-of-sale promotions, telemarketing, sales promotion, etc.

The psychology behind IMC is simple. Retention of messages (memory) depends on three factors: the clarity and simplicity of the message, the number of mental and emotional triggers attached to the message, and the number of times the message is repeated.

Benefits of Integrated Marketing Communications

In spite of the real obstacles to consistency and coordination, the benefits of IMC are well worth the time and money involved. A sound brand strategy will raise a company's brand equity and worth in the marketplace (price/earnings ratio), providing financial security for those with company stock or stock options. The right sales messages will move inventory out of the warehouses and into the hands of customers. Quotas will be met. Objectives will be achieved. The phones will ring when customers are surrounded by persuasive messages, appearing at the same time and in a consistent manner. IMC builds careers and helps companies grow to become market leaders.

IMC extends the reach of the traditional ad budget, provides a substantially improved marketing communications return on investment, and balances short- and long-term corporate needs. It improves agency and internal marketing productivity, tightens communications focus, and strengthens brand identity. Most importantly, customers perceive a clearer brand image of the company and its products.

IMC Tools

The basic tools of integrated marketing communications are as follows:

• Great advertising. Advertising is the lifeblood of brand building.

• Product packaging and/or product design. While a book should be more than its cover, it's vital that the box, package, chassis, and product look good and feel good to the customer. Spend more than you think you can afford. I've never seen a company spend too much on "the cover."

• Public relations. For smaller companies or companies with a limited budget, public relations should be number one in this list because it is so cost-effective and builds credibility through third-party endorsements.

• Direct marketing. Direct marketers are rapidly picking up on the importance of brand. Why? Probably because they are so results-oriented and can see the immediate value of brand associations to their selling packages. Embed the brand association linked to product purchase in every direct marketing piece that goes out, not only to increase response but also to contribute to the growth of brand equity.

• Channel promotion. Creating effective sales tools and properly training and motivating the channel is smart promotion.

• Price promotion. Price promotion is important, but it should not be used to the point where it devalues the brand. Strong brands enable you to milk the brand when you need short-term sales, while overused promotions start the spiral of demarketing, and demotion.

Next, let's look at the most important tools—advertising, packaging, public relations, and direct marketing—in more detail.

Brand Advertising: The Good, the Bad, and the Ugly

There are good brand advertisements and there are bad ones. Some are so bad, they're ugly! Here are some basic criteria for evaluating brand advertisements:

The Good

- Prominent brand name and logo
- Clear differentiation with clarity
- Consistent look and feel
- Incorporates brand associations on both concrete and emotional levels
- Impact—stopping power
- Believable
- High recall
- Strategic

The Bad and the Ugly

- Where's the logo?
- No one clear message
- Price only
- Ad-of-the-month club—every ad looks different
- Seeing an ad as a cheap way to do a data sheet
- The company talks to itself
- Strictly tactical

The Power of Advertising

Advertising can be immensely powerful. "In our business, I know the correlation between effective advertising and profitable long-term growth isn't 50 percent, it isn't 75 percent, it is 100 percent. In 22 years I have not seen a single P&G brand sustain profitable growth for much more than a year without great advertising," says L. Ross Love, vice president, advertising, Procter & Gamble Worldwide.[4]

In general, the use of advertising to reinforce customer purchase decisions and build loyalty is underutilized. We tend to put all our attention on new product introductions and neglect to care for all the loyal buyers who are just as insecure as new buyers. Notice whether you become more interested in reading ads after your next major purchase of a computer, software, car, or other major purchase at work or at home. Don't you read the ad for the brand you just purchased? Aren't you looking for more information to make you feel you just made the best and wisest purchase decision?

Advertising is about selling and communicating. Behind those goals lies the need for learning and remembering. The experience of abruption, a surprise or something different from what is expected, gets our brain's involuntary attention because the brain's job is to classify, understand, and determine if something is important to us.

There is an inverse relationship between the expectation of a stimulus and the intensity of the response and the number of repetitions needed to achieve the response. The more expected the stimulus, the less intense the response and the more repetitions that will be needed. The less expected the stimulus, the more intense the response and the fewer repetitions that will be needed.[5] This is basic psychology.

What this means for advertisers is this: If you take more risk with your advertising, i.e., do something unexpected and different, you can spend less on advertising to get your brand message across. If a safe look and message mean more to you, be prepared to spend more to get the brand built.

Advertising helps build perceived quality, reinforces the customers' experience of quality, and lets you command higher prices. Combining improved quality with increased advertising efforts can result in market share increases of 8 percent.[6]

In spite of the trend toward individualized marketing and diversity of media, if you ask high-tech marketers (or packaged-goods marketers), most will tell you that carefully targeted advertising remains the surest way to build and maintain market share and brand franchises. If you think about the relationship of advertising spending to market share, it makes sense that your ad spending as a percentage of the total advertising expenditures in your product category (your share of voice) should be at least equal to your percentage of market share to maintain share. If you want to grow your market share, your share of voice ad spending should be substantially greater than your market share. It is certainly worth checking these numbers for your company and your competitors in the market(s) you serve to see how the dynamics of advertising expenditure and market share interact.

According to The Arcature Corporation (a research firm), "Compared to market followers, market dominators allocate 26 percent more of their advertising and promotional budgets to advertising. Our evidence is unequivocal. In fact, while dominators spend half of their budgets on advertising, followers spend about 60 percent on promotion."[7]

The problem with tracking the effect of gradual budget cuts and underspending is that the downturn in sales, market share, and profitability is gradual. Like a long train or supertanker coming to a stop, the historic investment in brand building has a momentum that may hide the effects of reduced brand investment for months or even years. The problem then becomes, how do you get the supertanker up to speed again? Once you have lost customers and sales, you may never be able to regain the heights of success you once enjoyed.

Bill Gates and Advertising

Most companies don't spend enough on advertising. Are you spending enough? Here's a story about how Bill Gates learned the importance of advertising to Microsoft's growth. When he was president of Doyle Dane Bernbach in San Francisco, Jerry Gibbons had the opportunity to sell a billionaire-in-the-making on the value of advertising. Yes, one of the agency's new clients in 1981 was a new kid on the block, Microsoft. Early in 1982, since he hadn't yet met Bill Gates, Gibbons set up a meeting through Microsoft's marketing director.

As Gibbons tells the story, he was to meet Gates at the Airport Hilton in Los Angeles. Prior to the meeting, he asked his account group, "In addition to just meeting Bill, what else should I try to do?" They said, "Well, the reality is, they're not spending as much on advertising as they should be spending at this time."

At the time Microsoft's ad budget was about $250,000. The DDB account people told Gibbons that software was a burgeoning industry and that sales in this category would continue to grow at double-digit rates. "We should convince him to spend at a level that's appropriate."

So, in addition to meeting Gates and establishing a good client relationship, Gibbons' mission was to convince him to increase the advertising budget. "He was very gracious," Gibbons said. "We met late in the evening—about ten o'clock—had a drink, and were just sitting and talking, and I said, 'By the way, our feeling is that you're not spending at a level that's appropriate for your company right now.'

"He said, 'Why should we spend any more money?' So I took a bar napkin and drew a circle, and said, 'This is your industry today.' I drew a piece of pie in the circle and said, 'This is your current share, and as you know, the industry is going to be growing,' and I drew a larger circle, to represent the difference between $1.5 billion and $5 billion, and said, 'This is how it's going to be growing in the next few years, and good strategy for your company would be to capture as much share of market as you can now while the share points are cheap. Share points are cheap because the market size is small. As the market grows, the cost of acquiring share points is going to increase greatly. If you can increase your share, then when it becomes more competitive, all you'll have to do is protect your share.'"

Gates's reaction? "He grasped that concept very quickly." He went back to Seattle and practically doubled his advertising budget.

Packaging Sells

The quality of a product's packaging or "trade dress" (name, symbols, type style, color, overall design) is extremely important when the product is displayed on a retail shelf. Tide, Cascade, and other best-selling supermarket brands represent the epitome of carefully researched packaging. The package makes the first impression and represents the essence of the brand. Good packaging should perform a number of duties: be recognizable (a family friend told me she has been using the same feminine product for many years, yet she can't remember its name—only what it looks like on the supermarket shelf), stop the prospect, involve the customer on both a symbolic and an emotional level, clearly articulate the brand's position and associations, functionally protect the product in shipment and in use, and be ecologically responsible.

"It may not make much sense to do lots of four-color packaging for a product sold through a direct response channel because, by the time the customer sees it, they've already bought it," states C. E. "Charlie" Pankenier, IBM director of brand management. "On the other hand, in the retail environment, the package is an essential part of an integrated marketing communications approach, including the sales experience. So I may need to invest relatively more in the packaging in order to make the package work as hard as it needs to on the sales floor."

During 1993 Borland worked on redefining its message and establishing a stronger brand identity by tying the company name more clearly to each of the products. According to Heidi Sinclair, vice president of corporate strategy for Borland, as part of this program, Borland changed its packaging because it needed more powerful packaging, with an updated look. Before, you couldn't even see Borland on the packaging, and now it's big and bold. Before, each product had its own distinct look, and now they all look like part of a family. In order to establish an extended brand identity across product lines, start with a common look to the packaging.

Borland hasn't been able to track sales specifically tied to the new packaging because, during the same time period, it also lowered prices and did a number of other things. Even though Borland hasn't been able to link sales to any one change in particular, Sinclair says, "unit sales have gone way up."

In order to develop the new identity, Borland hired an outside packaging consultant. "We did a lot of mock store displays, and from that we knew that there were a couple of things that worked: Having a pretty simple background; yellow with black worked really well," Sinclair says.

Borland also spent a lot of time talking to channel customers to see what kind of packaging they liked, what worked, and how it should be displayed. Each of them has different displays, so it's important to design a package that is going to work in an Egghead store, which is laid out differently from other stores. Every side needs to sell.

The best way to get market share is to build on your strengths, leverage the brand as much as possible, and sell as many branded products from your whole product line to your loyal customer base. One popular way to do that is product bundles or suites, which bundle a group of products into one package. "You're essentially giving away the other products," Sinclair admits, "but you're working to buy market share because there's such a strong upgrade business now."

Bendix brake division of Allied Signal, East Providence, Rhode Island, learned the importance of packaging the hard way. Several automotive aftermarket chains refused to carry the Bendix brand because the packaging was not visually appealing for the stores' do-it-yourself customers. In response, the company conducted a brand-image audit, which revealed a haphazard use of color, logo, and look and feel. Bendix repackaged its entire brake line for the consumer market, using the color blue as a brand identifier, with the goal of making a stronger merchandising statement at point of purchase. According to Tom McCarthy, product manager, "For two chains alone that earlier refused us, sales are now in excess of $20 million. We've gone from a less than 1 percent share at retail to more than 20 percent. That's incredible growth."[8]

Public Relations and Direct Marketing

In your public relations, make sure that all news releases contain at least one association, write case history articles about happy users to reinforce a brand association, and use infographics to demonstrate brand associations as part of a press kit. Employ visuals, such as your corporate logo, to reinforce your brand identity, and subtly build associations into quotes and copy. Press kit folders, news releases, and other documents should have the company or product logo prominently and consistently displayed.

In direct marketing, collateral and sales promotion materials follow the same strategies used in PR: embedding brand messages into direct mail letters, flyers, videos, and commercials. Some direct marketers object that spending more time portraying brand image means spending less time making an offer and hence lower response rates. This is true. Brand imagery for imagery's sake is not the answer. What is important is to use messages and images that not only make offers, but take a longer-term perspective and build equity at the same time.

In a *Journal of Direct Marketing* editorial entitled "How Important Is a 'Brand' in Direct Marketing?" Don Schultz cites three reasons for direct marketers to consider including brand building in their direct marketing mix: (1) our culture's change from verbal (reading) to visual communications, (2) a reliance on the sound bite that makes us instant experts, and (3) declining consumer risk in the marketplace as most companies now back products with warranties and money-back guarantees.[9]

Build a database and record customers' demographics, buying habits, and needs. Use that information to deliver individualized messages. Even a simple "thank you" program can help retain customers. Track each relationship to continually evaluate media expenditures and what's working and what's not. Monitor the cost of acquiring the customer, as well as the lifetime value of the customer's purchases. Set up loyalty programs to reward frequent and regular buyers. Consider giving top customers a credit or "dividend" for buying future products or services.

A Model for Building Brand, One Step at a Time

IMC theory is great, but how can you apply it, test it, and measure results? Let's look at a model for building brand relationships at each step of the buying process. For many years, marketing communications programs have been built on the AIDA model of buying, which says that customers go through a series of steps to buy a product: awareness—interest—desire—action. One problem with the AIDA model is that the primary emphasis is on selling to new customers. A primary role of advertising and marketing communications in general is to reinforce the relationship people have with brands, not just get them to choose the brand. Your top priority should be to keep the customer sold. Gaining new customers is important, but secondary. Ignoring the relationship you already have with a customer while pursuing a prospective relationship you don't have is folly.

A relationship is not made at the wedding or the first sale. We go through a series of steps to build and maintain a relationship of trust. Here is one picture of the relationship-building process, with equal emphasis on pre- and postsale steps, as articulated by Phil Herring of Herring/Newman, a Seattle-based direct marketing agency: No awareness—awareness (have an opinion)—active interest (take action to find out more information)—research (make commitment to buy)—trial purchase (purchase and evaluate)—shared-use customer—preferred-use customer—exclusive-use customer. I would recommend adding "advocate" after exclusive-use customer. Champions for the brand create powerful word-of-mouth campaigns among the unaware, thus turning the process into a self-perpetuating circle.

Each of these steps presents an opportunity to gain a loyal customer. Appropriate communications at each stage in the process help the customer along the road to becoming an exclusive-use customer.

There are two types of loyalty: internal or emotional loyalty (I buy because I like these people) and external or rational loyalty (I buy because it's a smart choice). Loyalty begins when we genuinely care about customers, and it becomes a part of your culture when the loyalty is mutual and is perceived as mutual. One of the best ways to demonstrate caring is to ask customers what they want. Listen and act on what you hear. Ask them, What kind of offers would you like to receive? What ways and media would you like us to use to communicate with you? How often do you want to hear from us? How do you want to talk to us? Thank your customers for their feedback. Keep them involved.

Evaluating TechnoBrand Creative

After you've integrated the brand into marketing communications, how can you check to make sure you've done it effectively? When you evaluate a brand image or identity, ask yourself:

- Are there enough messages and clues to get the desired brand identity across?
- Do customers feel it is "my kind of brand"?

- Can it relate to one of Maslow's five levels of needs: (1) physiological (food, warmth, and shelter); (2) safety and security; (3) belongingness, love, and affection; (4) esteem and status, sense of importance; and (5) self-actualization?

When you evaluate a preliminary concept, ask yourself:

- Is it driven by a single idea that is deeply rooted in the customer's experience of the product?
- Is it abrupt enough to break through the clutter?

When you read a headline, ask yourself:

- Does it stop the reader with a believable promise in a memorable way?
- Does it work with a great visual to communicate a unique idea?

When you look at a visual, ask yourself:

- Is it essential to the message?
- Does it get stronger with age? Does it work harder on the third exposure than the first?
- Does it capture the drama in the product and establish an emotional tone?

The Emerging Revolution in Interactive Media

In *The One to One Future,* Don Peppers and Martha Rogers predict that we will work in a vastly different business and media environment. They write, "The 1:1 future will be characterized by customized production, individually addressable media, and 1:1 marketing, totally changing the rules of business competition and growth. Instead of market share, the goal of most business competition will be share of customer—one customer at a time."[10]

Look at the media. It used to be ABC, CBS, and NBC, period. Now TV watchers zap through a zillion cable channels, watching multiple shows concurrently. It used to be that everybody read the newspaper. Now newspaper readership is down to less than 70 percent of U.S. households.[11] It will continue to decline. Mass markets used to be easy to reach. Now, the challenge is to get to individual customers in a one-to-one economic system.

For example, Kimberly Clark, the manufacturer of Huggies diapers, has a personalized letter, magazine, and coded coupon system and maintains a database with the names of over 75 percent of the expectant mothers in the United States to establish long-term relationships and capture the $500 to $1,400 of disposable diapers that an average baby consumes annually. What distinguishes relationship marketing from other marketing communications is its purpose: to build long-term customer involvement and increased usage over time.[12]

While the $138 billion advertising industry is currently unprepared for a digital, interactive world where people can talk back to their television sets, the multimedia deal-making race is on. While it's true that ad agencies are not running over one another to hop on the interactive bandwagon, interactive technologies are still in the development stage.

What media should brand managers be researching and, if appropriate, experimenting with now? The advantage of being early into a new medium is that you capture the mind share of early adopters, who have a huge effect on the growing numbers of users who follow behind them. What will this interactive landscape look like? Interactive cable channels will enable viewers to walk down a mall of video storefronts; they will be able not only to see their favorite video movie, but also to shop for automobiles and other merchandise. Interactive kiosk catalogs will guide shoppers through the merchandise available in a store. A Seattle agency, the EvansGroup, helped create the "SeaFirst Wall," a "wall" of video monitors where consumers can interact with bank tellers and take care of just about any banking or financial transaction. Expect to see more "walls."

Lots of other interesting variations are being tested, such as movies on demand. The big opportunity for advertisers in interactivity is the chance to get real-time data on who watched the commercial, when, and how they reacted. Of course, all this assumes that consumers will really want to get up off their couches and interact with their televisions. And the cable and telephone companies acknowledge that the United States won't be wired for the electronic information superhighway for many years, although it is already well down the highway.

The world of interactive television doesn't necessarily mean the technology to avoid advertising. It also enables viewers to select advertising (e.g., "I want a PC, so I think I'll look at some PC advertisements"). This fundamentally changes the way advertisements are constructed, since they don't need to grab attention. Current experiments in this new era have been dubbed "infomercials." In the United Kingdom, Ford has moved to a straight news studio set with a "reporter" discussing, for example, the car's safety features. While this format undoubtedly reduces commercial production costs, will it build essential brand values—the deep-seated emotional desires in the consumer's subconscious value set, the determinate for preferring one brand over another?

Why should you use interactive media? Interactive media places psychological control in the palm of the prospect. Customers can shop when and where they want, selecting the products and services that are of interest to them. It can help you get new customers by explaining your services and products, improve service to existing users, and, at the same time, allow you to build a database and measure advertising success.

At the center of these new media is the ability to start and maintain a relationship with individual customers. Here is a synopsis of some interactive media that offer fresh and powerful means for building TechnoBrands one customer at a time.

Voice Technologies

Voice technologies use the telephone (or telephone lines) to gather data or help the selling effort. They are interactive and navigational, which means that the customer can get information, individualized to his or her specific needs, about a product or service and the company can build a database based on the individual's own choices.

Fax on Demand or Interactive Fax Systems

This system enables callers to use their Touch-Tone phones to choose information that will be sent instantly to their fax machines. The 1990s are the impatient age. We want to know now. Just look at the explosion in the sales of fax machines, which forced Western Union in 1991 to close down its 150-year-old telegram business.[13] A U.S. invention, initial market research found no interest in a machine that cost a lot of money to send a page quicker than the mail. It was the Japanese, watching the market explode for courier companies like DHL and Federal Express, that realized the potential. When positioned against courier services rather than a telephone extension, sales took off.

Interactive fax systems keep caller logs and statistics on the caller's phone number, the literature requested, and the source of the lead, which can be used to track advertising effectiveness and build a database.

Interactive fax can increase revenues while increasing the effectiveness of your customer service. Merisel charges suppliers to have their literature on its Fax-on-Demand system. Another company, Symantec, was losing 60 percent of calls after new product announcements. People calling in for new product information weren't getting their calls answered. According to Larry Miller, Symantec customer service director, the Fax-on-Demand system installed in 1991 received 25,000 requests for information in the first seven months, saving more than $60,000 in equivalent labor.[14]

Automatic Call Routing

This telephone switching system allows intelligent routing of calls anywhere in the country. Automatic call routing is one of the new enhanced voice services, or EVS, that major telecommunications companies such as MCI offer.

Here's an example: Instead of just routing the call to a customer service representative on the next floor, the system automatically reads the caller's phone number via Automatic Number Identification (ANI), locates the dealer nearest to that prefix, routes the call to that dealer, and announces via a special tone that this is a call from the 1-800 number. If the dealer's line is busy or does not answer, the system will take the call back and reroute it to the next closest dealer.

Caller Profiling

After a caller's phone number is identified via Automatic Number Identification, a database of households and businesses can be accessed to provide demographic data, including the name, title, gender, and age of the head of the household, the type of dwelling, how long they have lived there, a wealth rating, whether it is in an urban or rural postal code, and which Area of Dominant Influence (ADI) they are in.

Interactive Voice Response

Using a Touch-Tone phone, the caller can access a variety of information via a voice menu. Voice response makes complicated technology (the computer) as simple as talking with a friend over the phone.

Text, Graphic, and Video Interactive Services

The information highway represents the future of selling because it breaks through the traditional barrier of "one-way selling" to let prospects interact with your product when, where, and how they want to. Most important, a prospect can immediately and easily make a purchase.

On-Line Services

These services offer informational and interactive messaging, data gathering, marketing, and advertising using text, data, and graphics. For example, Prodigy is an on-line information, entertainment, and shopping service accessed via the personal computer that offers graphics-based marketing. Other on-line services include CompuServe, America On-Line, and the true beginning of the information superhighway, Internet, with 20,000,000 users and growing at the rate of 20 percent per month.

E-mail is growing very rapidly, thanks to Internet. This huge network of networks all around the world is where the bulk of traffic is flowing on the electronic superhighway. E-mail addresses are appearing in advertisements. A marketing communications manager for an electronics company told me that the company has eliminated direct mail to one of its markets; all communications are being sent via E-mail since most of the target market, engineers, are all connected to E-mail and use it frequently.

Electronic Bulletin Boards

These are set up to take incoming calls from people who have a computer modem and communications software. There are thousands of public access bulletin boards in the United States. The growth of bulletin boards operated by private companies has outstripped the growth of public bulletin boards. Bulletin boards are being used as twenty-four-hour customer service lines, where clients can get information, leave messages, or place orders. Limited access bulletin boards are used to transfer data between corporate headquarters and brand offices or the field sales force.

Two-Way TV

In January 1992, the FCC authorized the use of part of the radio spectrum for two-way, television-based interactive video and data services. Hopeful providers promote a variety of applications, such as playing along with game shows and sporting events, paying bills, viewing infomercials, requesting immediate attention by clicking on a "call me now" box on the screen, and, of course, buying goods and services directly.

CD-ROM or Disk-Based Catalogs and Brochures

Product and service information or interactive advertising is stored on CD-ROM or computer disk and accessed via a personal computer. If you print the words "diskette enclosed" on the outside of an envelope, the number of people who take the diskette out, pop it into the computer, and play it is almost 90 percent. While 1 to 2 percent response rates are the norm for direct mailings, electronic brochures frequently draw more than 12 percent response.

The benefits of brochures-on-disk include customer involvement, instant feedback on results, the gathering of a wealth of information, and the image impact of a new technological medium. Sometimes an "extra value," such as a game or a helpful software tool, is also included on the disk. Plus, really good electronic brochures will be copied and passed along to friends.

Electronic software catalogs on CD-ROM that are filled with lots of software programs from competing publishers are just beginning to appear. You can browse through the programs or try out trial versions that are crippled. If you see one you like, you can call a toll-free number and get a code to unlock the encrypted full version of the software and copy it to your computer's hard disk. While early software catalogs are less than ideal, count on early flaws being overcome.

The market is out there. The 1990 U.S. Census indicates that 68 percent of the population has access to a computer at home or at work. Additionally, 63 percent of the households with an annual income of $75,000 or above own a computer.

Studies have shown that people retain 10 percent of what they hear, 30 percent of what they see and hear, and a full 60 percent of what they do. Interactive disks are dependent upon someone doing something. And, in this environmentally conscious era, it is important to note that few people will throw out the disks they receive. Most people watch them a few times and then reuse the disk.

In 1990, Honeywell created an electronic sales pitch for its Explorer series PC-based process control system. The program led the user from product description to a simple breakdown of the computer's complicated hardware. It guided the prospect through the system, suggested which model would be best for him or her, and explained costs. The program allowed the user to respond to a number of questions similar to that of a warranty card questionnaire. Responses were printed out and sent back to Honeywell's database. The three-month campaign generated more than 1,500 sales leads, doubling previous trade ad results, and drastically improved the efficiency of sales calls. Just months after the ad ran, Honeywell had responded to nearly 12,000 requests for disks.[15]

In 1990, the Netherlands Foreign Investment Agency (NFIA) sent a disk to executives of high-technology companies. The goal of the campaign was to position the Netherlands on the short list of companies considering operations in Europe. The response rate for the campaign exceeded 10 percent. Of those who received the disk, 85 percent looked at it, 60 percent spent more than five minutes with it, 20 percent spent fifteen or more minutes looking at the information on it, and 70 percent rated the information useful or very useful.[16]

When considering a disk promotion, make sure your audience has access to a Macintosh or a PC and that your product is expensive enough to justify the cost of a using a disk-based medium. Keep it simple. Do surveys to find the technical configuration that will show your product best, but will also work on most people's computers. It is especially important to make the programs easy to load and fast. As in any direct response program, include a call to action (consider using the disk as the return piece and gathering market data at the same time). Don't forget a well-written, friendly sales letter and well-designed mailing package.

Using Timing to Your Advantage

Too many product introductions are done at the last minute with only the minimum of planning. If you begin the planning process early in the product development process, time can work to your advantage and allow you to get better and longer-lasting results. The place to start is to decide on your objectives and then put an action plan down on paper.

Take a look at Figure 7-1, the "Nine-Month Countdown to a Healthy, Happy Product Delivery." Recommending a *nine-month* product launch plan to a room full of high-tech marketers might bring forth a few choice cynical comments. That's why "The Four-Month Alternative. . ." is also given, in Figure 7-2. Somewhere between the two is the planning horizon for most high-tech marketers. Both those countdowns present a model outlining the sequence of events for a successful product launch: what you should do and when.

In implementing IMC programs like these, it's important to: take the time up front to research, plan, and develop brand strategy and messages; start the PR process far enough out so that the

(*text continues on page 162*)

Figure 7-1. Nine-month countdown to a healthy, happy product delivery.

The Four Month Alternative...

WE RECOMMEND

THIS COUNTDOWN

FOR UPGRADES AND

LINE EXTENSIONS.

BRAND
STRATEGY &
COMMUNI-
CATIONS
PLANNING

Prepare
& Finalize
Marketing
Comm. Plan

Product
Positioning
& Brand
Associations

-4 months -3 months -2 months -1 month ▶ INTRO

PR	PR Planning	Create Press Materials	Press Tour	Mail News Releases & Place Review Units	Editorial Coverage Appears
ADVERTISING & DIRECT MAIL	Establish Creative Platform ◆ Prepare Media Schedule	Concepts, Layout, Copy, Photography ◆ Obtain/Prepare Mail Lists	Ad Production ◆ D.M. Production, Printing	Place Insertion Orders ◆ Mailing Services	Ad Campaign Appears ◆ Installed Base Receives D.M. Package
COLLATERAL & CHANNEL ROLLOUT		Literature & Dlr. Materials Concepts	Copy Reviews, Layout & Photography	Production & Printing	Literature & Dlr. Materials to Field

Source: Floathe Johnson.

Figure 7-2. The four-month alternative.

Nine -Month Countdown to a

WE RECOMMEND
◆
THIS COUNTDOWN
◆
FOR MAJOR NEW
◆
PRODUCTS.

	Family Planning	Conception			
	-10 months	**-9** months	**-8** months	**-7** months	**-6** months	**-5** months

	-10	-9	-8	-7	-6	-5
BRAND STRATEGY & COMMUNI-CATIONS PLANNING	Market Research ◆ Prepare Marketing Plan	Prepare Intro Comm. Plan from Mktg. Plan Objectives	Conduct Positioning & Brand Associa-tion Research	Determine Desired Position & Associations ◆ Intro Comm. Plan Revised & Approved		
PR				Plan for Press Coverage ◆ Prepare Article Outlines	Create Press Materials (Bkgndr., News Rel., Q & A) ◆ Call Publica-tions on Cover Opportunities	
ADvertising			Creative Platform & Key Consumer Message Established & Tested	Ad Concepts ◆ Research Media	Concept Testing ◆ Media Plan Complete	
Direct Mail					DM Package Concepts ◆ Research Lists	
CHANNEL ROLLOUT	Establish Relationships With Key Resellers; Learn Their Needs & Systems	Prepare Market Development & Co-op Plan	Set Up Strategic Alliances	Packaging Concepts	End-User Literature & Channel Intro Materials Concepts	Copy Reviews, Layout & Photography for Intro and Co-op Kits

Healthy, Happy Product Delivery.

					Birth	Joy	Reality
-4 months	-3 months	-2 months	-1 month	INTRO	+1 month	+2 months

		Benchmark Research					
Media Techniques Training/Review ◆ Article Rev. to/from Editor ◆ Place Review Units	Sched. & Prep. Agenda for Press Tour ◆ Articles/ Cover Photos Complete	Press/Analyst Tour ◆ Follow-Up Calls ◆ Mail News Rel. to Monthlies	Mail News Release to Weeklies (1 Week Prior)	Editorial Coverage Appears	Rave Reviews & Leads ◆ Inquiry Fulfillment	Begin Placement of Application Stories
Ad Copy, Layout & Photography (inc. PR Photos) ◆ Finalize Media Schedule	Ad Production	Place Insertion Orders (Monthlies) ◆ Filmwork to Monthly Publications	Place Insertion Orders (Weeklies) ◆ Filmwork to Weekly Publications	Ad Campaign Starts	Calls & Leads Begin to Pour In ◆ Inquiry Fulfillment	Advertising Continues
Negotiate/ Order Lists ◆ Copy & Layout, Photography		Production, Printing	Mailing Services	Prospects, Installed Base Receive D.M. Package	Phones & Mailboxes Jammed With Leads ◆ Inquiry Fulfillment	Second D.M. Drop
Plan Road Show ◆ Select Cities and Book Facilities	Promotion Strategy for Road Show ◆ Strategize With Key Partners For Their Intro Success	Sign Dealers for Road Show ◆ Production, Printing, Collation	Deliver Dealer Kits	Road Show Promotion Begins	Road Show & Follow-Up	Analyze Sell-Through and Adjust Comm. Planning

Source: Floathe Johnson.

PR can break before or at the same time as the advertising begins to appear; and plan channel rollout carefully.

Integrating marketing communications is complex, often involving many departments and people, budget and time constraints, rigid timelines, multiple agencies, and sometimes other groups or companies. Yet, the nine-month countdown is being used by many market leaders today to their competitive advantage.

The real driving factors to true integration are the product development and marketing communications timelines that detail when activities start, which activities are dependent on others, and exactly when each element needs to be in place. Recognizing the following factors is also key:

- *Start slowly.* If you aren't using timing to maximize the return on your communications investment, adopt the total quality management principle of "continuous improvement." Begin to make small changes to your product launch timelines to enable you to compete more effectively.

- *Implementing IMC is not easy.* Getting multiple managers, agencies, consultants, and vendors to use the same words and pictures in a consistent manner requires diplomacy and extra administrative time. Skilled practitioners are a rare breed. Large agencies supported by the media commission system are often at odds with an integrated approach, and many small agencies lack the mixed-discipline backgrounds needed to put it all together.

- *Focus on the customer by thinking how you personally would want to be sold and serviced.* Improve coordination and cooperation between engineering and marketing when planning product development and marketing communications timelines and processes.

- *Try an IMC plan.* Evaluate the results and, as a team, look for improvements that can make each new product launch better than the one before. Finally, be alert! Brand building, IMC, and timing are major competitive weapons.

Charisma

Don't lose sight of what IMC is all about: building trusting and emotional relationships with customers, or charisma. Charisma is a key component of creating an inspired brand image.[17] Charisma is the quality of a brand derived from its presumed connection with emotional, relationship-building, and spiritual-imbuing powers. It is the basis of a brand's power to have a strong influence over the status or ideology of the target market. Charisma is all about loyalty, devotion, hope, trust, and faith in brands. In other words, eager and evangelical followers. Think about *Star Wars,* Nike sneakers, Marlboro, and Macintosh.

How do you build charisma? Use symbolism and archetypes. Choose brand associations that are emotional and compelling metaphors of prestige, the sacred, the transcendent, and that which is highly desired. Why do 77 percent of teenage boys in America want Nikes? It just might be because they've been repeatedly encouraged to "Fly Air Jordan" out of the inner-city slums.[18]

When planning your IMC program, think of your Techno-Branding efforts as a wishing mirror. What image can you create that your customers want to see when they look at themselves in the mirror?

Notes

1. Kevin Goldman, "Repetitive Ads Keep Viewer Recall Going," *Wall Street Journal,* April 7, 1993, p. B5.
2. Alecia Swasy, *Soap Opera: The Inside Story of Procter & Gamble* (New York: Times Books, 1993).
3. Don E. Schultz, Stanley I. Tannenbaum, and Robert E. Lauterborn, *Integrated Marketing Communications* (Lincolnwood, Ill.: NTC Business Books, 1993), book cover and xv.
4. L. Ross Love, "Back to Basics: Up with Advertising," A.N.A. Advertising Issues Forum, San Francisco, Sept. 13–15, 1992.
5. Burt Manning, "The Creative Equation," A.N.A. Advertising Issues Forum, San Francisco, Sept. 13–15, 1992.
6. Larry Light, "Trustmarketing: The Brand Relationship Marketing Mandate for the 90's," The Coalition for Brand Equity.
7. Larry Light, "Trustmarketing: The Brand Relationship Marketing Mandate for the 90's," The Coalition for Brand Equity. Used by permission.

8. Elinor Selame and Greg Koligian, "Brands Are a Company's Most Important Asset," *Marketing News*, Sept. 16, 1991, 19.
9. Don E. Schultz, "From the Editor: How Important Is a 'Brand' in Direct Marketing?" *Journal of Direct Marketing* 5, no. 4 (1991): 5–7.
10. Don Peppers and Martha Rogers, *The One to One Future: Building Relationships One Customer at a Time* (New York: Currency Doubleday, 1993).
11. Booz-Allen & Hamilton Inc., New York, "Relationship Marketing—Positioning for the Future," undated.
12. Booz-Allen & Hamilton Inc., New York, "Relationship Marketing—Positioning for the Future," undated.
13. Don Peppers and Martha Rogers, *The One to One Future: Building Relationships One Customer at a Time* (New York: Currency Doubleday, 1993).
14. Keith Prince, "Interactive Fax as Marketing Tool," *Marketing*, October 1993, 15.
15. Gary W. Wojtas, "Exploring New Response Avenues," *Direct Mailing*, February 1991, 44–46; "Electronic Brochure Doubles Honeywell's Response," *Direct*, Feb. 10, 1990, 29.
16. "Enticing Them with Interactive Diskettes," *Business Marketing*, August 1990, 25 and 28.
17. Norman Smothers, "Can Products and Brands Have Charisma?" in *Brand Equity & Advertising*, ed. David A. Aaker and Alexander L. Biel (Hillsdale, N.J.: Lawrence Erlbaum Associates, 1993).
18. Donald Katz, "Triumph of the Swoosh," *Sports Illustrated*, Aug. 16, 1993.

8

Creatively Implementing TechnoBranding

"People don't read brands, they recognize them. Strong brands have an identity."

Mike Isaacson, director of corporate marketing
Sierra On-Line, Inc.

"New products start with the same level of name recognition and benefits associated with the familiar 'parent' brand. This is good if the brand is strong in awareness and perceived value, but may be a detriment if the brand has negative connotations associated with it."

Michael Kelly, president of Techtel Corporation

At some point, the ideal world of TechnoBranding meets the real world of deadlines and decisions. There are political and cultural issues in every company, a brand name needs to be chosen in the next several weeks, and debates arise about product versus company brands.

As technology marketers recognize the importance of building their brands, where can they turn for help? Unfortunately, they face a Hegelian dialectic! The German philosopher Hegel introduced the idea of a "synthesis of opposites." When one idea, concept, or thesis is put side by side with its opposite (the antithesis), a new synthesis is created, which is synergetic or greater than the sum of the original ideas.

High-technology companies face a Hegelian dialectic in that their high-tech marketing and product managers, who understand well the technicalities of their products, are not equipped with the overall brand expertise and experience that their companies need but find hard to define. Finding talented and experienced Techno-Brand managers to lead the way through the unknowns of brand warfare is difficult and chancy. It is further complicated because brand techniques have either been viewed as proprietary trade secrets or, worse yet, have been only loosely applied and utilized, through ignorance. When looking for help, be sure to ask consultants and agencies, "What is your process for building brand, and what case histories can you show us?"

On one hand (the thesis), there are specialist high-tech marketing managers and advertising agencies who can talk technology with engineers.

On the other hand (the antithesis), there are P&G-type brand managers with reams of sales data and detailed promotion plans, and great mainstream advertising agencies that understand consumer branding techniques—but don't necessarily know which techniques are applicable to technology products.

To date, advertisers have viewed this as an either/or decision, while agencies have viewed the extremes as the ends of a continuum and debated where to position themselves on the continuum (running the risk of a gray compromise).

The synthesis (of apparent opposites) is the recognition that high-technology branding not only borrows from but *differs* from consumer branding.

TechnoBranding represents a definition of this synthesis by building technology knowledge with consumer branding into a new school of marketing. At the least, there is an urgent need to educate advertisers, as well as advertising agencies, on how to develop brands for technology companies. Hence the development of the TechnoBranding process, which is itself a brand. Practically speaking, the process represents the technology for building brand for any business or product. It applies the latest in communications and psychological thinking to branding.

Which Comes First, Brand or Corporate Culture?

Most brand marketers define and build a brand on top of a product and then half-heartedly comment that the internal corporate structure ought to live up to the promises made. In many cases, the corporate culture is the brand (Apple, IBM, Microsoft). This is an argument for building or starting with the existing corporate culture first.

Changing corporate culture as a means of creating a brand is a good idea for technology companies that forgot their customers, lost their way, and now have to "change." In any case, the brand needs to be perceived as credible by customers. You can't have brand advertising saying "customer care" if customers keep getting busy signals or being put on hold when they call for help.

One of the most important, and indeed vital, elements of communicating TechnoBrands is employee buy-in and understanding of what the company stands for in terms of customer interaction. What an exciting idea! Consider employees as a key element in brand building. When hiring new employees, tell them what the company stands for and that they will be expected to represent, contribute to, and be a part of the corporate brand. Before starting such a practice, proceed cautiously. Explain that the company wants to present a consistent image and "personality" and get employees' reactions and buy-in beforehand. Internal newsletter, customer newsletter, and company publication editors have a close relationship with employees and customers. They should be considered important members of the brand-building team.

Because attitudes follow behavior, customer service training is a basic building block of a brand campaign. Teach employees how to encourage customers to try out products. Ask experienced car salespeople how important a test drive is to the sale. It's common sense that if people get their hands on the actual product, especially with some help from a savvy salesperson, a good percentage of the "test drivers" will at least consider a purchase.

Take a look at your company. Are the beliefs, values, images, and customer-perceived behaviors of your company, as a whole, consistent with the image of the company's products? The closer the fit between what the company and the product brands stand for, the more likely it is that brand equity will be maximized.

If the values or image of the product do not fit its customer-perceived company image, the company brand should not be used. Brand use has limits. Did you know that Tylenol is a subsidiary of Johnson & Johnson? Because the brand name Johnson & Johnson is used only on its baby and family products (e.g., Johnson & Johnson Baby Shampoo), the rest of the company was able to come out of the Tylenol disaster with hardly a scratch.

Institutionalizing Brand at FWB

When a company is building distribution channels, image and identity are "very important," explains Steve Goodman, vice president of marketing and sales for FWB, a manufacturer of mass storage and backup peripherals and related software. FWB relies on resellers to deliver products to customers, and considers the company and its products' brand identities as key in recruiting and keeping resellers focused on its line rather than competitors'.

Branding is especially important with highly substitutable products. "My 600-megabyte hard drive doesn't hold any more megabytes than somebody else's 600-megabyte hard drive, so in terms of pure functionality and capacity, our products are highly substitutable with those of our competitors," he explains. Thus, FWB needs to rely on branding.

Key attributes for FWB are reliability (essential for a storage product), performance, power, and a high level of comfort regarding the perception of how much support is available, how easily accessible it is, and how quickly and effectively it's delivered. The relative importance of attributes can shift as conditions change. At FWB, performance, service, support, and expectations are on the rise. It isn't just that the product doesn't break, but that it's backed up with more than adequate support staff who are accessible and deliver support and service quickly and effectively.

Goodman is a strong believer in institutionalizing the brand. Make the brand values very clear and known up and down the organization so that everybody's singing the same tune, understanding what those values are, and working together to enhance the brand value.

Goodman concludes, "In our company, everybody plays a part

in continuing to add to our brand equity" for Hammer, FWB's storage and backup hardware, and for Toolkit, a group of related software products.

TechnoBranding Service Businesses

Not all companies manufacture and market products like FWB. Many are service firms. What are some tips and guidelines for service businesses? The basic problem when marketing services is to transform the service from an undifferentiated commodity to a branded, value-added product. All service companies want to be perceived as better than their competitors. The solution is to make the company brand distinctive and relevant in the minds of clients. Because a service is inherently abstract and intangible, the importance of research and careful positioning cannot be overstated. Then, use visual symbols to make the service more easily understood and remembered (e.g., Allstate's good hands, Prudential's piece of the rock, Travelers' umbrella). Once you find a good image, stick with it. Don't change it. Ever. Merrill Lynch made the mistake of retiring its bull image, but was quickly forced to bring it back.

What's in a Name?

A good brand name gives a good first impression and evokes positive associations for the brand. It is said that Steve Jobs, founder of Apple Computer, picked the name after visiting the All-One Farm in Oregon because, to him, the apple is the perfect fruit and he wanted Apple to be the perfect company.[1]

Brand name recognition is valuable and almost priceless in a cluttered, competitive market. Selling a product with a new, unknown brand name is like rowing a boat upstream. If you aren't one of the top three brands in a category, you're anonymous.

Criteria for Brand Names

Here are some important factors to consider when choosing a brand name:

• Available and trademarkable. The cost of getting brand names is increasing because it is getting harder and harder to find available names that haven't been trademarked. Start with a long list, and don't get attached to one name early on. If it's that good, chances are it's already taken. Be prepared for at least two rounds of trademark searches, unless you have created a new word for your brand name. The trademark search is an important step in the naming process. Your brand name is compared to those already registered with the federal or state government. Common-law searches of Yellow Pages and other directories are also useful. It is much less expensive to do a comprehensive search up front than have to change your brand name in the future because another company had prior rights to the name. Get professional and legal help for the trademark search and registration process.

• Different and distinctive, yet simple and easy to remember. Why pick a name that's either close to a competitor's brand name or hard to pronounce or spell?

• Meaningful. Pick names that suggest the category, industry, or product. Try to get a name that evokes desired brand associations and doesn't suggest undesirable ones.

• Test with customers. Don't omit this step. Customers associate things with names that insiders never expect. If you don't ask customers in a focus group setting what they think of certain names, and what they like and dislike, chances are you will pick a name with negative baggage.

World Names for TechnoBrands

"An important trend among large companies is the adoption of a single brand name which can be used unchanged around the world," says Ira Bachrach, president of NameLab, Inc. of San Francisco. Since the economic integration of Europe and the globalization of markets, it's become not only impractical but silly to sell one product under different names. Bachrach says that's why marketers are combining existing national brands under one international name; for example, Whiskas, a European cat food name, was made into a world brand by Mars, Inc., replacing Kal Kan in U.S. markets.

"The most effective world brands have turned out to be short new words based on English-language morphemes . . . like Sony," Bachrach explains. The reason is that these types of brand names are easy to say, easy to read (they are spoken as spelled), and visibly proprietary.

Being "visibly proprietary" is easier said than done in a world where the majority of people don't read languages written in the Roman alphabet familiar to Americans. According to Bachrach, that's why international marketers particularly treasure words that incorporate proprietary "flags" like a doubled letter (Exxon), initial-terminal consonance (Xerox) or assonance (Acura), or an echoing repetition (Coca-Cola).

Bachrach gives several examples of successful brand names. A joint venture of Goldman, Sachs and several other international finance firms needed a world name for an ambitious international electronic trading system that would allow governments and dealers to trade government securities. The name had to say that everyone can see every transaction at the same time on computer screens worldwide. As this was to be a genuinely world system, the name could not be perceived to be American, but it had to be based on English, which is the international language of high finance. NameLab named the system Univu.

When an American company developed a piece of software that made it much easier for computer users to scan and edit photographs, they required a world name expressing the message "scanning and editing photos is easy and fun." NameLab developed Ofoto, which now identifies the product in many nations.

When Sun Chemical and Chromalloy American merged into a multibillion-dollar conglomerate, NameLab created Sequa, a world name for the new company, to suggest long-term planning—a philosophy that Norman Alexander, the founder of Sun Chemical, used to maximize shareholder value.

"In a computer store like CompUSA [another NameLab name], a customer faces thousands of identities—brand names and companies fluttering about his head like moths," Bachrach observes. "Rather than create new coined names for new products, we often end up recommending that a client in the market reduce their inventory of coined names, integrating products into a single brand with new SKUs [products] identified by simple, comprehensible language like 'Fast Database.'"

Bachrach's TechnoBranding rule of the 1990s is "less is more."

"The fewer coined brand names a company has out there, the stronger each brand will be," concludes Bachrach. "It's as simple as that."

Brand Names at AT&T, McCaw, and Cellular One

What do you do when a company with very well known brand names acquires or merges with a company with its own brand names? Usually the dominant company and brands win because the equity of its brand names is greater and it makes sense for the company with weaker brand names to gradually shift to the new brand name.

A case in point is the merger of AT&T with McCaw Cellular Communications, which markets its cellular phone service under the Cellular One brand name. "One of the great drivers for us in the merger with AT&T was the ability to use AT&T's brand," states Robert Ratliffe, vice president, corporate communications, McCaw Cellular Communications. AT&T is one of the most recognized brands of any kind and is certainly the most widely known brand in telecommunications. Because the telephone is the lifeline of business and an integral part of daily life, people look for a telecommunications company, product, and service they can trust. AT&T stands for trust, loyalty, quality, and reliability.

"AT&T looked at Cellular One and said they wanted to keep that brand as well," says Ratliffe. McCaw is in the midst of talking to customers and noncustomers about how to use both brands, if that's appropriate, and how to get the most out of them. Ratliffe says if you ask people to list the top three providers of cellular, four out of five will list AT&T. (AT&T isn't even in the cellular business.) "We've talked about naming our North American cellular network 'The Cellular One Network brought to you by AT&T Cellular,'" says Ratliffe.

Ratliffe's advice for creating new brand names is, don't limit yourself by the brand. "Because our industry changes so rapidly, we wouldn't have called ourselves McCaw Cellular if we had to do it again," Ratliffe explains. "We wouldn't have attached an individual's name to it, and we wouldn't have called it cellular. At one time, we were called McCaw Personal Communications; we should have stayed with that. We don't have brand loyalty as McCaw. We have brand loyalty as Cellular One."

Don't let ego drive your brand name selection. Always have the customer drive your selection. Ideally, pick a brand name that is a descriptor and isn't confusing. "If you look at our competitor US West, they started out as VectorOne, then they were NewVector, then US West NewVector Group," Ratliffe says. "Nobody knows what NewVector is. But people will say, 'I have one of those US West Cellular One phones.'"

While we're talking about a brand name based on an acronym, AT&T, it's important to make it clear that acronyms should be avoided when naming a company or a product. Some people looking for brand names think that because AT&T, IBM, and other acronym-based names are successful, they should have a three-letter name, too. This is a big mistake. A lot of the power in the AT&T brand name is there because people have known it for a hundred years, literally all their lives. Most companies don't have 100 years to build a brand identity and can't begin to match the investment that AT&T and IBM have made in their brand name. The case against acronym-based brand names can be won by looking at the Fortune 500 list of leading companies. Note all the three-letter name companies you never heard of. That's because letters are really hard to remember. Instead, pick a name with meaning, symbolism, and rhythm. It'll be much less expensive in the long run.

What's in a Logo?

Your logo can be as important as your brand name. Research the effect your logo has on customer perceptions of your brand. In one survey, almost half of the logos tested were found to actually detract from and send negative messages about the images of their respective brands. This disturbing data suggests that you include logo perception testing in your brand research program. Also, make sure that your logo, which is so extensively used in all communications, isn't a dragging anchor for your brand's image.

"While I was at Nike, the creative people got tired of looking at the Nike logo and started fooling with it—doing Nike in script,

changing colors, making new designs with the swoosh, and changing the packaging," says Mike Isaacson, now director of corporate
marketing, Sierra On-Line, Inc. "We went through a period of two
to three years [in the mid-1980s] when our brand awareness was
on the decline. That may or may not have been the reason, but we
decided that this made no sense; we had an identity, and we decided we shouldn't mess with it."

Company Brand versus Product

What's more important, promoting company brand awareness or
product-specific advertising? This is one of the most debated issues within technology companies. Both company and product
brand names are important. With TechnoBranding, there's no reason you can't communicate brand messages in all communications.

The Debate at Logitech

Logitech is one company that has been wrestling with the question
of whether to brand the company or the product. Vanessa Torres,
pointing devices marketing manager, says the debate is based on
the fact that most technology companies look to the packaged-
goods industry as their model. For example, if people think about
baby diapers, they think "Huggies," not the name of the company
that makes them. "For us, if people think about our mice, they
think of Logitech," Torres says. "They can tell you the color of their
mouse, but they can't tell you that they own MouseMan, which is
the brand name."

Logitech believes strongly in branding and plans to continue
branding the company because it is trying to expand beyond mice
into imaging and sound products. It hopes that when people see
the Logitech name on a new product, the positive associations of
the Logitech brand name will transfer to the product.

Marketing manager Bill Mowry says that the importance of
establishing a strong company identity became clear when Logitech broke into the sound market. "We felt the Logitech brand
would have quite a bit of impact in that market, yet it's specific to

certain markets—pointing devices and imaging solutions. At the beginning, it was difficult to break through that mindset."

Mowry says that Logitech's first two sound products, AudioMan and SoundMan, haven't sold as well as expected. With SoundMan, he believes the reason is that there wasn't enough differentiation. "Now," Mowry say, "we're in the process of releasing a whole family of products, and I think that will have a much greater impact. The fact that we have a full product line will give us more visibility on the shelf and make us a bigger player."

The Logitech brand stands for innovation in products and quality. A key component of quality in the PC market is support, which Logitech makes available seven days a week. Support is important with entertainment products. Even though people generally play with their entertainment products on weekends, they still want immediate gratification. If a consumer has trouble installing the product and can't get help, he'll take it back to the store on Monday.

Logitech plans more comprehensive promotional plans that will go across product lines and will be customized for each specific product. Enter another variable. "We consider ourselves a 'senseware' company (we've got the hands, we've got the sounds, and we've got the sights)," Torres says. "We're going to have to make another choice: Are we branding the senseware or Logitech?"

Competing against Microsoft is tough for Logitech because of Microsoft's financial resources. "They have more money than we're ever going to have," Torres states. "They spend more on their mouse products than we spend on our entire line of products." To compete against a market leader, you have to fine-tune your point of difference. Rather than ignore Microsoft, Logitech acknowledges Microsoft's position and directly compares Logitech and Microsoft mice. Introducing Logitech's new MouseMan Cordless product, the advertising said, "In May Microsoft introduced their new mouse, and in June we introduced this mouse. We think it's better and we want you to try it." Logitech added an aggressive offer that people didn't need to pay for it for sixty days. "We actually got letters from people who had a Microsoft mouse and took it back after trying ours," Torres says. "We didn't sell a lot more mice directly, but our sales have tripled on the product. You've got to get the product in the hands of the people who are the advisers (they're the ones who bought direct, I'm sure), then they'll tell their friends, and those friends walk into the store to buy."

One thing Logitech doesn't fear is taking risks with its advertising. Some of its advertising is very controversial (one Logitech ad shows a naked baby boy urinating), and there are raging internal debates about it. There have been some calls from people who say they'll never buy Logitech products again, but at the same time, people have asked for their most controversial ad to hang in their offices because they love it.

"It's all subjective," confesses Torres. "If you want people to think of Logitech, it's working. If you're a product manager, you probably are unhappy because no one remembers what the ad's for."

For a campaign for a mouse software upgrade, the company switched from the controversial approach to product benefit ads. The campaign was successful; revenue goals and target numbers were met. Is it contradictory to praise controversial advertisements on the one hand, and product benefit ads on the other? Yes. In the real world, we all have to live within the context of other people's decisions and make the best of it. The best-case solution would be to carefully track brand awareness, consideration, and loyalty over time and test the controversial and product benefit advertising campaigns in order to know what's best.

"The grocery industry can tell you how many Pepsis are being sold a minute and what influenced that, but this industry today isn't there yet," Torres says. "We have a lot of proprietary research being done to measure our brand against the competition, but we're paying a hefty sum to get it. For branding to really be a big part of the technology industry, we're going to need some of the tools to help us with it."

Adobe Postscript—Linking the Product Name To the Company Name

Adobe Systems, Inc. linked the company name to its popular Postscript software for the first time in an advertising campaign launched in 1993, years after Postscript had been well established among select markets. The ads feature a magnifying glass highlighting the Adobe name.

Two factors drove the development of the campaign. While the Adobe brand name has a very good reputation among Macintosh users, graphics publishers, and printer manufacturers, it is not well known in the PC market. People who had heard of Postscript not only didn't know what it was, they didn't associate the name with Adobe.

"We felt it was important to raise awareness of Postscript, particularly in the PC community," says Debra Triant, Adobe's vice president of marketing. "And we wanted to brand not just the name, but the logo itself, for two reasons: One, the logo is much more memorable than the name itself; two, Postscript is an open format—a published format." An open format is good for customers, but another consequence is that other companies can make Postscript clones. Adobe wanted to link the company brand, Adobe, with the product brand, Postscript, and have people look for Adobe Postscript. While competitors can use Postscript, they can't use Adobe's logo. Within the industry, Adobe has always stood for the highest-quality product, so Adobe wanted to turn the logo, the brand's symbol, into a seal of quality.

Adobe also recognized the importance of making sure that when people look for a printer, they see the symbol that the advertising has encouraged them to look for. So, Adobe started a detailing and dealer education program. Adobe representatives went into the top 1,200 retail outlets (in terms of printer sales), put tent cards on top of the printers, and attached laminate cards that identified them as Postscript printers—using the same image used in the ads, the magnifying glass with the logo under it.

"The feedback from dealers is that they noticed a surge in interest and questions about Postscript in the first weeks of the detailing effort," reports Triant. "We're tracking sales in the stores where we've done the detailing, but from the start, the anecdotal evidence has been very strong."

The foremost goal of the branding was to drive the demand for Postscript, but Adobe also did it for its OEM customers. "Our OEM customers have been very happy about the campaign as a whole," Triant states.

Triant believes that in the software industry, the brand name of the company, while secondary to product, is more important than in consumer goods. The company name says something about the overall quality and reliability of the products and the likelihood that the company will continue in existence.

"The brand name can go against you as well, as soon as there's a perception that it's outdated or that the quality isn't there," Triant concludes. "When you have a quality brand name, you have to take care to make sure that you're doing right by the customers and that they will continue to value that."

Branding the Product Rather Than The Company Name

Walker Richer & Quinn (WRQ), publisher of Reflection brand communications software, has chosen to brand its products rather than the company name. One reason, according to George Hubman, former vice president of marketing, is that "We don't sell any Walker Richer & Quinns. People have a devil of a time with 'Walker Richer & Quinn.' Some people remember 'WRQ.'"

WRQ changed its corporate identity a year ago, with a conscious objective of continuing to develop Reflection as the brand name and to reduce Walker Richer & Quinn. When the telephones are answered, the company is identified as "WRQ Reflection."

"We branded our product 'Reflection,' and we've sold the hell out of it and have at this point an incredibly high level of brand recognition," Hubman says. "I think we could take a lot of different products and put the Reflection brand on them at this point, and they'll be successful. If it addresses their needs, they will buy it." When you are well known and respected in your key market segments, people will buy whatever you produce until you prove that you've sold them a crummy product.

WRQ has even listed telephone numbers in the Seattle directory for Reflection software. Service people—both tech support and people in the sales organization—will return phone calls and identify themselves as being with "Reflection Software" because they're that sure that the person knows who Reflection is.

Brand Extension

Building new brands involves risks and expense. As the huge feature differentiators of the past fade and technology enters a more commodity-like field, superior brand management becomes the differentiating factor. So, if you have the choice of building a new brand yourself or acquiring an established brand from another company, look to buy the established one, if the price is right.

Is it any wonder that companies rely on brand extension to capitalize on the awareness of their current and successful brand names that is already in place when they introduce and name new products? Since 1987, 70 percent of brands, about 24,000 all together, produced line extensions.[2]

How do you keep the brand name growing? One way is to break the parent brand into chunks and create separate product line brands, or child brands, to represent them.

If the brand name has been taken far enough, it's time to create another category. For example, Nike has created cross-training, water sports, outdoors, walking, multiple basketball segments—Air Jordan (Michael Jordan), Force (David Robinson and Charles Barkley), and Flight (Scottie Pippin)—and multiple tennis segments—Challenge of the Court Collection (John McEnroe and Andre Agassi) and Supreme Court.

Brand extension eliminates or reduces the need and expense of naming and conducting extensive name test marketing. It also offers a cheap means to get a product onto the shelves.

Brand extension is also one of the most important ways of leveraging brand equity. "What you want to have is strong brand equity: solid value, a solid impression in people's minds of what your company stands for," says Dave Roberts, worldwide advertising manager for Claris Corporation. "It sounds like motherhood and apple pie, but it's fundamental to effective marketing."

If people have a strong idea of what Company X stands for—customer support, ease of use, power, reliability, etc.—then when that company rolls out a new product or a new category, its marketing expenditures are going to be much more efficient and its opportunity for success much greater. People will say, "This new product is being produced by Brand X, and I know and like what that stands for."

One exception to the power of brand extension is when the brand name has virtually become a generic word (e.g., "Hand me a Kleenex"). In cases such as this, brand extension works against the brand and devalues it because the image, the illusion of synonymy, has been taken away, and the magic begins to fade.

Since unsuccessful brand extensions are costly, make sure the current brand name is extendable to a new product category by checking the criteria in the following section and, most importantly, by research.

Factors for Successful Brand Extension

Some brands work only in one category (Coke soft drinks). Some brands work only in one area of expertise (Lotus's 1-2-3 spreadsheet software). These strong brands, high on the ladder of awareness, should stay close to home and harvest their profits in their parent category. Conversely, weak brands with little brand equity need more brand building before they can be leveraged and extended.

It is always easier to extend brands to closely related categories than to distant categories (e.g., the Peter Norton brand name seems to equal any kind of utility software). This is because the customer needs to believe that the brand is a logical fit in the new category and that the brand brings a benefit that is wanted in the new category.

Therefore, the new "child" brand should be consistent with, and complementary to, the "parent" or "mother" brand. There should also be a good perceptual fit and benefit transfer. Like clothing, new brands must fit and look proper on the parent brand.

Make sure the associations of the parent brand are desired by customers in the new category and that no negative associations are formed by extending the brand. The extended product should be equal to, or better than, competitive products in the new category. Consider the risk of the extension diluting or changing the meaning of the parent brand. For example, adding "plus," "extra," or "ultra" to the brand name may cause buyers to switch to the new brand at the expense of the parent brand.

Brands based on quality claims (e.g., reliability, performance) are more extendable than brands based on specific associations.

However, because quality associations are general, they won't extend as far as a specific, very relevant association will if that association is valued in the original as well as the extended market. For example, with Ivory soap, because "pure" is a quality association, it is more extendible than the specific association, "It floats." But think of the equity in the Ivory brand name that P&G can leverage as it extends Ivory out of the soap category and into the cleaning products category. In most cases, though, it is rare to find that one association is rated number one in two different categories.

The best idea is to always go back to how the brand is perceived and defined by the customer. Through research, find out what products the customer will give you permission to use with the brand name. Is there a logical and psychological fit? What are the brand's characteristics and boundaries? Can they be leveraged? To find out, ask customers for the new product category if they want these characteristics and if they value the brand's current associations.

Brands Have Limits

It's also possible to add to customers' confusion if you're not clear about how they perceive you. "You need to have a tremendous understanding of what your brand stands for; once you go outside of that, you confuse the consumer," says Mike Isaacson, director of corporate marketing, Sierra On-Line, Inc.

Also, it's important to realize that customers may think a brand stands for something other than what the company thinks it stands for. "Nike, for example, may describe their brand as standing for high-quality apparel and footwear," according to Isaacson, who was with Nike for eight years, "but to customers it stands for sports footwear and apparel. Nike tried several times to transfer the brand to leisure-oriented products and had little success. If it isn't sports-related, the Nike brand didn't transfer well, so Nike started new brands for products outside sports."

Brands are powerful, but they have their limits. Unfortunately, the way most companies learn how far they can extend the brand is by trial and error.

Plan for success from the very beginning. When you are determining your brand, or naming your company or products, decide how far you plan to extend the brand.

"Stay true to the brand," advises Isaacson. Know what your brand stands for, and stay close to that brand definition, at least until the consumer understands that definition very well. Then, if you want to extend into other areas, spend the money to research the acceptability of extending the brand to that area. Research expenditures are much cheaper than a failed product and damaged brand image.

Brand Name, Research, and Extension at Microsoft

How important is brand to Microsoft? "Our number one brand, obviously, is the Microsoft name. It has been our most valuable asset," according to Marty Taucher, director of public relations for Microsoft. "And then, second to that, is our Windows brand, which we think is very important as well."

The Microsoft Windows advertisement in Figure 8-1 is an excellent example of brand advertising. The brand name, Microsoft Windows, is repeated six times. The brand association of "easy" is made powerfully and persuasively. This is not subtle brand building; this is blatant branding.

There are lots of debates within Microsoft on which attribute is most important: the Microsoft name or the individual product. Picking the right product name is an extremely important strategic decision for technology companies. Some software companies, like WordStar and WordPerfect, had to change their company names to their product names because the product became so successful that no one recognized the company name. This means that follow-on products are automatically associated with the first, which can be limiting as the company changes and grows.

"I think WordPerfect actually made a conscious decision to change their name to reflect their product name," comments Taucher. "For a company that wants to be more than just a single-product vendor, it's a challenging box to get out of once you equate your company name with your product. They get trapped into all kinds of troublesome areas by trying to come up with names like DataPerfect that are related to their primary brand name, but are not too successful. Other companies have done a good job in this area. I think Lotus has done a terrific job moving beyond simply a

(*text continues on page 187*)

Figure 8-1. Microsoft Windows advertisement.

Why do 9 of the top 10 PC manufacturers preinstall Microsoft Windows on their PCs?

(continues)

Figure 8-1. (*continued*)

Why are over 1 million copies of Microsoft Windows sold every month?

Why are 95%
of the people who
use Microsoft
Windows happy?*

(continues)

Figure 8-1. (*continued*)

The answer is easy.

Easy to install. Easy to learn. Easy to use. Easier than you can imagine.

That's how the Microsoft® Windows™ operating system version 3.1 operates.

Of course, ease-of-use means nothing without speed and reliability. Which is just what you can expect. And you can choose from thousands of applications that run under the Microsoft Windows interface.

But in order to really understand why so many PC users, computer manufacturers and software developers have fallen for the Windows operating system, you'll have to check it out for yourself.

Call (800) 426-9400 for the name of the reseller nearest you. You'll quickly see that nothing could be easier.

Making it easier

Source: Microsoft Corporation.

1-2-3 company. They worked very hard over the years to establish Lotus as a separate brand name, above and beyond 1-2-3, despite the fact that over the past five years 1-2-3 is 90 percent of their revenue. The fact that they've invested in the Lotus brand name has allowed them to diversify out of the spreadsheet business into word processing and workgroup software with Lotus Notes."

Microsoft is a company that decided a long time ago that it was going to be a company with multiple businesses. The primary investment was going to be in the Microsoft name, to establish Microsoft as the leader in the software industry with high-quality operating system and application software products. As the market has grown and expanded, new markets have emerged, such as the recent Microsoft Home consumer launch.

Microsoft has been closely associated in many people's minds with business software, so switching to consumer software products for the home is a major change. But, it's no surprise that Microsoft is moving to the home consumer market. Microsoft research shows that 40 percent of annual PC shipments will be for the home market and growth rates are projected to be 16 percent per year for the next several years. "We definitely see the computer as a household appliance, and we're doing everything to deliver products to meet the tasks of home users," explains Meg Metzger, a Microsoft marketing manager.[3]

"We've spent thousands of hours in research, listening and learning about exactly what type of software people want and how it might be useful to them," says Patty Stonesifer, vice president of Microsoft's Consumer Division.[4] According to Taucher, Microsoft has done a wide range of research, all the way from primary research about consumer attitudes and general feelings about personal computing to one-on-one interviews with customers and consumers. Microsoft hired a research company to do an extensive random-dial survey of households in the United States to find out if they use personal computers and what they want and expect in software for the home. They also did a lot of one-on-one interviews with customers and focus group studies to ask customers what were the kinds of things that, if Microsoft could automate them, would help make their personal lives easier. After a product has been designed and developed, they conduct usability studies to evaluate how the software measures up and to test product features with consumers by watching them interact with software behind a one-way mirror and recording their movements with the mouse and on the PCs.

What did Microsoft find out from all this research? "Home consumers are looking for a set of attributes that are different from Microsoft's traditional values," Taucher says. "Microsoft is associated with being powerful and easy to use, in terms of word processing and spreadsheet software. While consumers are not necessarily looking for power, they are looking for ease of use. At home, they're looking more for attributes like enjoyable, good value, and easy to use. So our efforts in the home market are going to stress the enjoyable and good value aspects of that product line."

Does Microsoft consciously embed these types of attributes and brand associations in its advertising? "Absolutely," states Taucher. "The advertising has to reflect the image of the company and the brand the company's trying to get across." All of Microsoft's ads are signed with the Microsoft name, so they're not like a Procter & Gamble ad where the corporate name is deemphasized for the benefit of the individual product. "We don't think that's appropriate or makes sense," states Taucher. "We think the Microsoft name has a lot of value to consumers. Over the years we've invested totally, both in advertising and P.R. and in all our marketing communications areas, to build up the Microsoft brand name, so we want to leverage that wherever possible. In time we want to be able to establish alternative brands which will mean different things to different consumers. For example, we're establishing a new brand called the Microsoft Office. But it is the Microsoft Office brand, not just Office."

How would Microsoft like its brand to be thought of in people's minds in, say, five years? "We have some specific objectives," answers Taucher. "In general, we believe we've achieved the mind share of the customers as seeing Microsoft as the leading company, not only in the software industry, but in the PC computing industry. We want to build on that leadership with a reputation for innovative products that make people's lives better, improve their overall productivity, and are fun to use, depending on which segment you're with. I think we'll settle for the worldwide leader in the PC industry, and being known for high-quality products that are very innovative."

"Microsoft has developed such a strong brand with such enormous awareness and such enormous credibility, it will be interesting to see how well they can do with the brand's extendibility," says Mike Isaacson, a competitor who's watching with great interest. "My personal feeling is that extending Microsoft into the gaming world is overextending the brand."

To defend against the competition from such an industry giant, Isaacson says, "There's no way you can match them money for money, but I'll bet on our game development people over theirs. Our marketing strategy will be to be the very best in particular niches. We'll be a powerful niche player, and they'll be the one with the overextended brand. Time will tell.

"There are a lot of different niches in the gaming world, and we cover some of those niches with some brands and some of those niches with others," Isaacson continues. Sierra On-Line is currently doing research to determine whether one of those brands can cover all of its niches so it can use the power of the brand to sell all the niches. "One of the research pieces that I think will be helpful is a correlational study—using enthusiasts only—to see what the correlation is between people who buy one niche and those people who buy another," adds Isaacson. If enthusiasts are buying both niches, then the correlation is high, and using one brand should not be a problem. If they're buying just one niche, then extending one brand may be a risk.

Isaacson believes that when you develop brands, you're aiming at enthusiasts—people who use the product day in and day out, who really identify with it. Each time you extend the brand to cover more market niches, you risk losing the enthusiasts in the niches you own. At that point you have to work harder to convince those enthusiasts that you remain the leader in their niche—even though you've extended that brand to other niches. You have to work harder to keep other companies that are aiming at that niche from coming in and knocking you off. When you say, "I'm no longer a specialist in that niche," you open the door for specialist competitors who want to come in and steal the leadership position away.

Organizing for Brand Management

A chapter on implementing TechnoBranding is not complete without a discussion of how a company should organize to manage its brands. The brand management system was started in the early 1930s by Neil McElroy on the Camay soap business at Procter & Gamble. In this system, the brand manager is the champion of the brand, and the ultimate protector and promoter of the brand both within the company and to all the customers. What do brand managers do? The short answer is, "whatever it takes."

A brand manager is the architect of the business, the business manager responsible not only for profit and loss, but for knowing everything about the product, from sales figures to legal issues. A combination team player, leader, and facilitator, the brand manager makes and defends budgets, develops marketing plans and strategies, and coordinates distribution and sales, all to keep the business growing as fast as possible. Like an entrepreneur, the brand manager manages the brand as if it were his or her own. As a consumer advocate, the brand manager ideally does what's right for the customer first, and what's right for the company second.

What's a brand manager's day like? Minding the store, the brand manager follows sales revenues and promotion results; tracks brand awareness, consideration, purchase, and loyalty figures; goes to focus groups and evaluates the quantitative research for ways to improve marketing strategy; and works with the channel and sales force. The brand manager spends a lot of time with the advertising and public relations agency, makes presentations, coordinates pricing and price promotions, deals with daily crises, and, in general, makes things happen.

Brand managers are important, but the trend is to brand teams. Brands have simply grown too complicated for one person to handle. Getting everyone connected with the brand to take profit and loss responsibility has vast repercussions on how people work. With a brand team management structure, the focus is on molding the business to customer satisfaction, not on the function. Planning is integrated, and the responsibility for the plan is shared. A coordinated team approach enables the company to respond quickly to market and competitive changes. Even more important, brand team management turns bureaucrats into entrepreneurs. People get involved instead of withdrawn, feel responsible instead of isolated.

Brand Teams at IBM

The IBM Personal Computer Company has switched to a brand team approach, with notable success. "We have recognized, for not just the PC business but for IBM in general, that 'one size fits all' is not the way to be successful these days because the customer is looking for a choice that is the best possible fit with their particular needs and wants in terms of function, price or where s/he prefers to buy," says C. E. "Charlie" Pankenier, IBM director of brand management.

Some people prefer to buy computer products through catalogs and direct mail. People who are relatively new to technology want the reassurance of knowing that when they buy a product, there is a person who will help them if they encounter any problems or have any questions. Within a large corporation such as IBM, how do you resolve the conflicts that naturally arise between departments in order to give the customers what they want how they want it?

"The notion of brand teams is a response to our recognition that the marketplace is highly segmented and you need to put together an offering that is not only the product, but also the way that you offer it, bring it to market, and sell and service it," explains Pankenier. That's true in the PC marketplace and all the way up the line through midrange computers to the large organization that's installing a global banking network. There are significant differences in those market segments. "As a company, if you want to be successful you must accommodate yourself to those preferences," Pankenier says.

Brand Management Considerations

Brand team management is not easy! It's a big job. Getting the right people is crucial. The team should be composed of people who can see the big picture and still handle day-to-day business details.

If your brands are not being adequately or properly supported, if your business is getting too big and complex, if planning is reactive instead of proactive, then brand team management will help focus a small group of managers on the business's success. Team management will enable restructuring for increased accountability and help the team meet customer needs, achieve business objectives, and keep the brand alive and growing.

If your markets are maturing, growth rates are slowing down, and dollars available for spending are limited, brand team management allows the employees closest to the business to work out the trade-offs, deal with the issues, and simplify the management process.

If people feel powerless and frustrated, give them the authority, budget, and responsibility to run their own brand business. They will take ownership of the business and realize that while running a business is a lot harder than they thought, it offers more rewards and fun than simply filling a job.

However, a purely brand-driven structure can create internal competition and internal customer interface systems that are counterproductive to building customer relationships, especially when a company has several subbrands under a "mother" brand umbrella, as HP does.

Perhaps a "best of both worlds" solution is a customer-oriented model in which teams of people surround customer groups or types of customers and promote the subbrands customers want in a synergistic way. "If you have a branding model, the team is rewarded for getting *their* brand in there, not doing the best overall job coordinating with the customer," says Derrith Lambka, corporate advertising manager, Hewlett-Packard. "A customer-driven company, with teams of people who understand a particular customer group, can make the internal organization transparent to the customer and make it easy for the customer to do business with you."

Who's the biggest brand manager of all? The CEO. The CEO is ultimately responsible for the biggest brand the company owns, the company itself.

Notes

1. Frank Rose, *West of Eden* (New York: Viking Penguin, 1990); John Sculley, *Odyssey* (New York: Harper & Row, 1987).

2. Ed Vick, "Brands on Trial," *ADWEEK*, May 24, 1993, 24–31.
3. Tim Talevich, "Microsoft Goes Home," *The Costco Connection*, November 1993, 27.
4. Tim Talevich, "Microsoft Goes Home," *The Costco Connection*, November 1993, 27.

9

Transcreation: Global Brand Building

"The challenges of managing brand globally are enormous. It adds many layers of complexity because of language, customs and cultures, and competitors you may not know about, but who are prominent players in specific countries. You have to be many, many times more diligent and thoughtful about the way you brand products globally."

Roy Verley, director, corporate communications for
Hewlett-Packard Company

For technology companies to succeed, they need to compete in a global marketplace. By the end of 1992, the United States represented only 35 percent of global information technology expenditures, and Europe represented another 35 percent. Many U.S. companies are finding that their growth opportunities are in international markets, particularly if their markets are saturated. The end result is that all the major technology companies are forced to operate in a borderless world.

All advertisers have, to a greater or lesser extent, tried to overcome the differences in language, demographics, laws, and culture that exist between countries. These national differences also apply to the manufacturer of technology products, and there are additional constraints as well. For example, product specifications and prices can vary dramatically from one country to another.

Technology companies that understand the power of the brand can overcome this dilemma. The point has been made in earlier chapters that people don't buy products, they buy brands—the values that the product and manufacturer represent to them. The marketing effectiveness of these values, unlike language, features, price, and promotions, is remarkably consistent across geographic boundaries. Basing advertising and company messages on the core brand values is the first step toward building a consistent global brand.

Creating a global brand that goes beyond a common look to become a part of industry or international culture is extremely difficult; it's hard enough to make a standardized product. It's far more practical to localize brands for different markets, countries, and cultures. The process is called *transcreation*, and because brands are largely intangible and perceptual, the process is a creative one, not just "drag and drop."

The key to transcreation: Tailor products to suit local taste and do research to verify correctness and appeal.

Localization is very important to the success of global brands. Customers in other countries live in a cultural world that is different from yours, so every brand needs to take into account the background of perceptions resident in each country or culture. While it's evident that different terms and words mean different things in different cultures, remember that different colors mean different things in different cultures, as well.

While the goal is great brand advertising that can transcend borders, what too often results is a lowest-common-denominator advertising campaign that doesn't work and is disappointing to everyone concerned. What's the answer? The fact is, there are no easy answers, only lots of hard work from researchers, country-knowledgeable marketers, and a willingness on the part of company management to not only take the time necessary to find the associations that will travel globally, but also create an environment for the advertising agency team that will result in a "highest-common-denominator" campaign.

Branding remains critically important in any market, but you can't assume that what is important in the United States is important everywhere. The French, the Germans, the English are all different. When localizing the brand, make sure local managers understand the key brand associations you want to come through, then give them the latitude to respond to conditions in their own market and encourage them to adapt.

On the one hand, you have rules about what ads should look like. Then, you start to bump into all the cases where that approach isn't appropriate, and you start to reduce it to a low common denominator. On the other hand, you define the core values that are the roots or at the heart of your brand. Then you allow it to grow and to change by encouraging local managers to add on a brand association and adapt the brand identity to appeal to the region's culture.

John O'Toole on Global Branding

Before you decide to launch a product in other countries, you need to be sure that the product itself has appeal and a reason for being there, taking into account that there are "vast cultural differences," says John O'Toole, past president of the A.A.A.A. "In my experience, household cleaning products, or utilitarian products, have a more global appeal than products that people use to make a statement about themselves, such as fragrances or automobiles."

Identifying a common appeal or benefit that can be spread across the world and determining the common marketing or advertising objective are the foundation for a global brand identity. "Often, advertising in execution may differ from culture to culture, but in objectives and strategies, it's either identical or similar," O'Toole says.

Name is less important than the symbology (i.e., the graphic identity, the promise, the benefit, the exclusive feature of the product) that goes into the identity. You can make name changes from culture to culture if you keep the brand identity constant. However, the verbalization of the name must take into consideration what the meanings and connotations of the language are in that culture. O'Toole cites the example of the Chevrolet Nova, which translates to "don't go" in some Latin languages. Obviously, that wasn't a good choice for a universal product name.

Tips for Global Branding

Start global branding by having a successful brand in one country. Bring the brand to birth in a country that is relevant and beneficial to the brand, not necessarily the one in which the brand is manufactured or was invented.

Value- or quality-based abstract associations are usually more transferable across geographic boundaries and different media than concrete associations like product specifications and prices. Focus on significant product features, mythology, and symbolism with universal emotional and human appeal. For example, when Applied Microsystems needed a brochure that would work in the United States, Europe, and Japan, Greek and Roman figures and architectural elements were used to create a sense of quality that would transcend national boundaries. Company representatives in each country were consulted early in the creative process to make sure that the concept not only would be accepted, but also would serve as the prestige piece needed to establish credibility with new customers.

"Speed to market is of the essence," says Michael Perry, chairman of Unilever, the world's largest advertiser outside the United States.[1] In competitive markets, once you create a successful brand, get it rolled out quickly and all at once. Don't take a gradual, conservative approach or your competitor may steal your idea and get it introduced in other countries before you do.

To be successful in transcreation, dedicate yourself to an understanding of the importance of human emotions and psychological fulfillment in brand relationships. Personal, business, national, and international relationships are built upon emotional and psychological factors, and they should be at the heart of every brand. A good example of human values crossing geographic and cultural borders is the Western as a film genre, which fulfilled a human psychological need of escape and freedom. The Western may have originated in the United States, but it has universal appeal. Not only were U.S. Westerns watched around the world, other countries started making their own Westerns. Italy was so prolific that it gave rise to the term *spaghetti Western*. Is it any wonder that the Marlboro Man is so successful?

Endorsements are a powerful way to build brand internationally. Music, sport, and movie personalities, because they travel and perform worldwide, can become a universal dramatic expression of the brand. Traits to look for in a spokesperson or character: worldwide recognition and visibility; an image, role model, and attitude that is relevant to your brand; and not only being in sync with the times, but having lasting appeal. A few examples of such personalities include the Pink Panther, Jerry Lewis, and Clint Eastwood.

Yet simple messages can usually be transcreated without the significant investment needed to license a character or hire a famous person as a spokesperson. Consider the techniques used to build the Microsoft brand association of "easy," expressed as their tagline, "Making it easier." The brand association of "easy" has been transcreated to European markets, with its different cultures and media. One U.K. TV commercial, supported with a poster campaign, features a grandmother gymnast easily going through a routine on the uneven parallel bars. A single, simple message is repeated in both high- and low-cost media.

Intel is another good example of transcreation. In the Intel "Vacancy" TV spot, a red arrow saying "Vacancy" is used to dramatize the message that Intel computer chips are upgradable. Upgradable means that the buyer's investment is protected and that the buyer will be able to run tomorrow's software as well as today's. Intel took a highly technical issue and put it in understandable terms. The same commercial ran in Europe with press ads reinforcing the message to "protect your investment," thus helping to create a truly international brand. In fact, the red arrow has been used through all promotional material, including direct mail and even point of sale.

The Intel Inside logo is also used throughout Europe on posters showing the logo over the numbers 486 in large type (proving that you don't need massive creative budgets once you have established a brand property). More importantly, the Intel logo also appears in most other PC manufacturers' advertising (not to mention on the front of the PCs themselves). If you need a clear example of how to image a technology brand, watch the Intel Inside TV commercials.

What can global marketers do when, in many product areas,

significant product improvements are hard to come by and, if they are found, are quickly copied by competitors? Does this mean that the unique selling proposition is dead? Yes. It has evolved to positioning statements and brand associations, and more sophisticated branding techniques for more sophisticated buyers. It certainly means that more focus is going to be placed on emotional branding. Japan has used such soft-sell techniques for decades, using surreal pictures and blatant emotionality.

Japanese consumer advertising relies upon mood—image-related, emotional, and nonverbal messages, which are more easily remembered than feature-oriented, logical messages. Part of the reason for this is cultural. Japanese consumers process information starting with a whole impression of the brand (e.g., is it good or bad?) as opposed to examining individual features first and then developing a total impression, as is common in the United States and Europe. For example, Japanese housewives go shopping every day or every other day and make many in-store decisions.

The Japanese emphasize developing market share and introduce new products frequently as a marketing strategy to help accomplish this. Hence, corporate familiarity and consistent tone and manner are emphasized in advertising. Corporate "mother brand" trademarks and logos are seen as key elements in brand building in Japan and, hence, appear more frequently than in the United States.[2]

Are the Japanese on to something? Is corporate brand building where it's at? The Japanese seem to violate all the rules about brand extensions and put the corporate name on everything from soap to floppy disks. Kao Corporation's research found that if they didn't put the Kao name on the disk, customers didn't buy them.[3]

Rules are only starting places in branding. If in doubt, check with the customer.

Veteran international marketers will tell you that advertising is the surest way to build brand and markets. To this add public relations, direct mail, event sponsorships, seminars, cultivation of opinion leaders. Distributors play key roles. The goal remains the same: Get customers to ask for the product by name.

Where is branding hot? In Asia, from China to India, American brands get big price premiums compared to the local competitors. This is because the United States is seen as a producer of high-quality goods, and those goods are seen as a way for other people to live the American Dream. For example, Johnson & Johnson baby shampoo and Band-Aid bandages command a 500 percent premium. Gillette razors go for twice the competition's, and Citicorp's premium credit cards go for an annual fee of $132 in Thailand. The sales and growth are there, too.[4] If Asian consumers are willing and ready to switch to higher-priced consumer brands, technology brands won't be far behind.

Notes

1. Noreen O'Leary, "The Hand of the Lever," *ADWEEK*, Dec. 14, 1992, 24.
2. Hiroshi Tanaka, "Branding in Japan," in *Brand Equity and Advertising*, ed. David A. Aaker and Alexander L. Biel (Hillsdale, N.J.: Lawrence Erlbaum Associates, 1993), 51–63.
3. David Aaker, "The Role of Corporate Brands," in John Berry, ed., "Brand Equity," *BRANDWEEK*, June 28, 1993, 22.
4. Patricia Sellers, "Brands, It's Thrive or Die," *Fortune*, Aug. 23, 1993, 52–56.

10

The Bottom Line

"Brand loyalty has never declined as much as the press
and folklore would have us believe."

Tod Johnson, president of the NPD Group[1]

"Only the top one or two brands in each category will survive in today's brutally competitive environment."

Reed Abelson, staff writer, *SmartMoney*[2]

In the past several years, the media have reported the decline of
consumer branding. Are brands really getting battered, or is it just
media hype? While some brands have lost value in the marketplace, the numbers tell a different story. *Financial World's* annual
ranking of brand values reports that thirty-five of 1992's top fifty-
nine brands rose in value in 1993.[3] In fact, their portfolio of brand
values rose 3.1 percent, while the economy only grew 2.2 percent.

What's the number one brand? None other than the Marlboro
Man is riding on top, with a worth of $39.5 billion. Second is Coca-
Cola, rising 37 percent in value from 1992. The key to Coke's success is leverage and brand extension, and its ability to sip every
ounce of value out of the Coke brand name. Intel, a high-
technology newcomer to *Financial World's* list of brand valuations
in 1993, entered the list at No. 3 with a valuation of $17.8 billion.

Whatever the state of consumer and TechnoBrands, comparing their financial trends is like comparing Coke to computer
chips. In general, consumer brands are mature and in stable markets, while technology brands are new, fast-growing, and entrepre-
neurial.

What's really behind media stories about the decline of brand values? The problem is not with the effectiveness and worth of brand identity. Corporations are certainly not perfect. And a number of them have made mistakes that cheapened their brand names, such as transferring marketing dollars from advertising to retail promotions and raising prices too often and too much, despite the fact that new technology on the manufacturing floor was making the process more efficient. Combine these factors with tough economic times and the high debt costs of expensive acquired brands, and you make it easy for consumers to trade down from the leading brand names and switch to alternative lower-priced brands.

The other side of the "fall of the brands" story is simply that advertisers have failed to do as good a job as they should in changing times. When the going gets tough, internal advertising and brand managers switch priorities from brand building to job security. The result: conservative advertisements with too much similarity to everyone else's.

The answer: Don't build up a big internal marketing communications staff, hire top talent internally to manage brand communications, reinforce their brand-building mission, and make personal relationships with the senior agency management on your account a priority. "Love thy agency, for only it can lead you to the land of great campaigns and share growth."[4]

Another big reason for the decline in brand values is that companies aren't spending enough to keep the brands' value high. Retailers have forced companies to spend dollars on trade promotions instead of advertising the products. And, while the many channels available through cable offer more choices to consumers, they also make it harder for advertisers to get their message through.

In the 1980s, even though inflation slowed, manufacturers still aggressively raised cigarette, soap, and cereal prices. Consumers, conditioned by years of advertising messages and encouraged by heavy promotion, still stayed brand loyal.

Then came the big and costly Kraft and RJR Nabisco takeovers. That did it. Brand prices became too dear, too high. Consumers spoke by cutting back or switching altogether, letting packaged-goods manufacturers know that their premium price limit had been reached and exceeded. Philip Morris, hearing the voice of the customer, cut the price on Marlboro cigarettes, which led to a large drop in the stock market known as "Marlboro Monday."

Once consumers move from exclusive use and switch, it's hard to win them back. The growing price disparity opened the door for new and improved private-label house brands to establish share. Recognizing the value of their own in-house labels, the supermarket chains became big winners. The reason is simple. Sales go up 15 to 20 percent because private labels look like real brands![5] They also generate higher profit margins for supermarkets.

Despite the defensive maneuvers by the big-name brands, supermarket sales of store brand goods continue to rise, while total supermarket sales are flat. Private-label sales account for 19.9 percent of all items sold in grocery stores.[6] National brand names are not going to disappear, but the times of fast and automatic profit are gone.

Retailers have some notable advantages over manufacturers: Their own computer-based cash registers can track sales quickly, their shelves become their market research department, and they don't need to build factories or do national advertising. What would you do if you were a mass merchant or a superstore? Perhaps emulate the supermarkets and establish your own private store brands?

What Can Be Learned from Battered Brand Headlines?

First, don't believe everything you read in the media. In a society filled with uncertainty and the need to adapt to new situations, brands continue to represent a safe choice, symbolizing an island of stability and reliability in a sea of change. Their battered image has been greatly overstated in the media. Second, watch the premium price you charge and don't let it get so high that buyers start switching, i.e., don't gouge customers on price. Third, keep your manufacturing process proprietary and as advanced as possible to inhibit copying.

Make a better product and continue to be innovative by increasing R&D and new manufacturing equipment spending as fast as revenues rise. Similarly, keep advertising spending on track with revenue growth. Or take advantage of the situation, and grow market share by increasing ad spending at a more rapid rate than revenues.

Brand-battering media stories deal with well-known packaged goods (e.g., Marlboro) and private label (e.g., A&P) brands. For technology and computer-related companies, brand is new and very much alive and offers a powerful competitive advantage to those who choose to use it. And, in an age of merger and acquisition, building your brand equity is literally building the market price of your company. To those high-tech companies who choose not to build brand, be forewarned that this decision may someday prove to be your death knell.

The keys to brand survival in the 1990s are to "price competitively, innovate brilliantly and market consistently."[7] Keep track of shoppers, stay abreast of changes in marketing techniques, keep promotions in check, integrate marketing teams with research and manufacturing, build better relations with the channel, develop new channels and delivery systems, and acquire brands that work across borders. All this advice for food marketers from *The Economist* applies equally well to technology brand marketers.

While the focus of media stories on brand has changed from how much Wall Street leveraged buyout specialists will pay for premium-brand companies to how much the customer will pay for the brand, reputation for quality is also more important than it used to be. According to a survey from Roper Starch Worldwide, who surveyed 2,000 Americans and compared the results to 1989 results, past experience with the brand remains the most important factor in buying decisions.[8]

What does this mean to your company? The basic lessons are these: Make it a priority to measure the brand's value at the customer level, and do that on a regular basis. Understand your brand's price elasticity, i.e., how far you can stretch the price before customers switch, and keep the price under that point. Allocate capital and manpower resources and sew a strong financial thread throughout the brand organization. It's amazing what happens when you start charging people for capital and resources. The company becomes more efficient.

Advertising Agency Brand Advice

To get the most from your brand, demand an agency team that has brand experience and make sure they stay on your account. Write that into the contract. Make agency agreements that are two or three years in length, not just for one year. Involve your agency. Get them out in the field and close to customers. Put your product in their hands. Get them involved in the marketing planning. Treat them as an investment, not as a cost; as a partner, not as a vendor.

Companies doing their advertising in-house should return to the use of outside advertising agencies and reduce the size of in-house operations. In-house operations do not have the objectivity and creativity that brand building demands. At the same time, higher standards for agency performance should be set. Many companies talk about measurable objectives and standards of performance, but few are willing to invest in even the basic systems needed to track results.

Keep everyone's eyes, including the agency's, squarely on the desired brand building results: sales, profits, market share. Create an environment that expects and loves great ideas and has the discipline to stick with a great idea once it is found.

How much is an inspired idea worth? How big can the return on just one great advertising idea be? Ask Microsoft about "Making it easier." Ask Intel about Intel Inside. Ask Philip Morris about the Marlboro Man. Ask McDonald's about "You deserve a break today." Ask Ivory soap about "99$^{44}/_{100}$% *PURE®—IT FLOATS.*" These are the ideas your agency should be accountable for creating.

The Importance of Brand Equity

Brand Equity Defined

Brand equity is the financial advantage of a brand over a generic or less worthy brand. The financial value of the difference between brand and product value is measured financially as the incremental cash flow that accrues from the linking of the brand with the product. If product alone is function, brand is the value that the name, logo, and associations add to the product. Software is much more valuable if it is from Microsoft, Lotus, or Borland. A computer is more valuable if it has Intel inside. Brand, then, is all the things a customer purchases.

The brand is an intangible asset on the balance sheet. Managed and nurtured, it becomes a significant asset. When Philip Morris acquired Kraft in 1988 for $12.9 billion, $11.6 billion was for goodwill, the majority of which was based on the estimated brand values.

If you have stock and stock options as part of your compensation, brand equity can multiply the worth of the company's stock. For example, in the fall of 1993, Microsoft's and Intel's price/earnings ratios were 31 and 34, respectively. Brand building helps make stockholders rich.

Brands also prime the pump for sales promotions when inventories are high or a company needs quick sales. Strong brands are the most profitable because they are perceived as high quality and they attract loyal, repeat customers.

How to Lose Brand Equity

Achieving brand equity is a lot like getting a line of credit. It's a lot easier to get it when you don't need it. If you ignore brand equity, you are liable to lose your best people and lose shelf space.

There are lots of ways to lose brand equity. Ignore and don't respond to competitive pressure. Neglect the brand. Don't move with the market. Don't move out of a declining market (e.g., the move away from Wang). Legal challenges (e.g., breast implants). Demarketing activities. Act of God events (e.g., Tylenol). Product failure. Overemphasis on short-term gains through price promotions. Negative associations. Inadequate integrated marketing effort. The easiest way to lose brand equity is to lose your image of quality (e.g., Schlitz beer). A long period of ineffective advertising or none at all may allow a brand to slip back into a commodity niche.

Just as maintenance determines the long-term performance of a car, proper maintenance of a brand is critical. It takes a long time to build a brand, so once you've got one, you need to handle it carefully. "Brands are like pieces of fine crystal; they take time to create and are easy to break," says Mike Isaacson, director of corporate marketing, Sierra On-Line, Inc. They must be handled carefully. You need to protect them, be cautious as to what you put next to them—and keep them out of the hands of children!

"There are brand equity-building marketing strategies, and even more opportunities to damage the equity you are working so hard to build and maintain," Isaacson says. "Equity builders must far exceed equity depleters."

Building Brand with Investors

Still not convinced that building TechnoBrands is a good financial decision? Salomon Bros. has advised investors to evaluate the marketing strength of computer companies as well as their technology.[9] Marketing expertise and brand equity will continue to become more important to the investment community.

Perception is reality. Rumor as well as fact fuels your company's market value. Shape reality or let it be shaped for you! While we tend to remember the high-flyer stocks and success stories, most initial public offerings end up below their offering price. To combat this and obtain a fair valuation in a merger, sale, strategic alliance, or stock offering, you must communicate with the press, customers, analysts, and investors as early and as often as possible.

Investors look at performance, corporate culture, the company's vision and business plan, the management team, and the overall finish or look of the company's marketing materials. To win over investors, treat them as a customer segment and consistently market to them, using brand associations as the brick and mortar of your communications. Supply key statistics on your business, market share, and industry to investors. Make their stock selection job easy.

To stimulate demand for your stock, identify and target the key market influencers. Then to get your fair market valuation, perform and communicate regularly and forthrightly. Increasing demand for your stock will make it easier to obtain private investments, form strategic alliances, make an initial public offering

(IPO), manage information during the post-IPO period, and sell your company.

Communicate your position, performance, strategies, and objectives by using a business plan or private placement memorandum. Communications attract desirable partners and alliances, which can increase your credibility—"validation by association."

Putting a Dollar Value on Your TechnoBrands

"Brand valuation is an area we are looking at," says Roy Verley, director of corporate communications for Hewlett-Packard Company. "The main value in having a valuation of your corporate brand is to understand just what an asset it is, and to convince management that it needs to be managed carefully like any other asset."

Brand valuations can be used for acquisitions and mergers, investor relations, setting royalties for brand licensing deals, tax planning, brand management, brand strategy planning, resource allocation, brand extension research, and good brand financial management.[10]

If establishing a value for brands sounds great, why are few companies doing it and how do people come up with different values? The best measure of brand value is what another company will pay for the brand. Of course, you don't want to put your brands up for sale every time you want to conduct an audit. In other words, there's just no easy way to value brands.

There is growing interest in the accounting for brand names and including them on the company's financial statements, especially in the United Kingdom. In the United States, brand names are typically lumped in with other intangible assets on the balance sheet under "goodwill," if they are included at all. Barriers to placing a value on brand names include establishing the life of the brand, identifying a formula that takes all the many variables of brand value into account, and the complications in auditing brand values. On the other hand, including brands as assets that are shown on financial statements could lead to better management of brands as assets and perhaps even a longer-term perspective to management decisions.

Begin to work with your accounting firm to value and measure brand equity. Explore accounting methods to measure the financial worth of the brand and forecast its future value. Then, test the method and resultant value for validity, repeatability, and auditability.

One of the most frequently used systems of valuing brands, according to Michael Birkin, group chief executive of Interbrand, is an earnings multiple system, where an appropriate multiplier is applied to the earnings of the brand.[11] The system is auditable and quick, and bases the value on hard data. The multiplier is determined by taking into account the brand's earnings (cash flows), the range of multiples within the industry, and the brand's strength (which determines the relative size of the multiple).

Putting a value on TechnoBrands makes it easier to raise capital and can increase the worth of the company in order to protect against takeovers. Consider mentioning and reporting on the importance of brand to the company in your annual report.

Finally, remember what John O'Toole says: "Even though there are formulas for establishing brand value, I think all of them miss the mark on the low side." So, don't underestimate the value of your brands.

Conclusion

If your business was going to be split up into two parts, with one part consisting of the brands and trademarks and the other part consisting of the buildings, equipment, and physical assets, which part would you choose? If you chose the brands, congratulations. If you chose the brick and glass part, maybe you should rethink why you're in business or where you're working.

TechnoBranding is the architecture and blueprint for building and maintaining brands. It delves into the depths of brand to a greater degree than most methods previously described or actually used. TechnoBranding is more than building brand image through advertising. It's a way to get the company deeply involved in the concerns and needs of your customers. And it forces your agency and creative resources to become intensely involved with your business and brands. TechnoBranding builds stronger teams within agencies and companies because it gives a common vocabulary and language for talking about brands and marketing in general.

As products have become commodities and tangible features become similar, customers begin making decisions based on intangible features. According to Laura Patterson, program manager for the "Powered by Motorola" campaign, Motorola has embarked on a brand-building program to communicate the intangible reasons for companies to work with Motorola: partnership, manufacturing capabilities, and the safety of working with a global, stable company. The goal of this brand-building effort is to influence the buy decision and create a feeling it calls the "pride of association" with Motorola.[12]

Pseudobrands based on pseudo values will fail. TechnoBrands are about honesty, morality, values, and, ultimately, spirit. You can't create emotional ties to bad products because that's dishonest, and customers find out and make you pay. Brands aren't about controlling customers. Brands are about getting in sync with customers, talking their language, and making their lives easier, better, and more fulfilling. Brands are about letting customers into the factory, letting customers shape the product, and communicating with them on their own terms.

You must take a stand. Declare yourself. And win customers' hearts along with their minds. Just because you make software or hardware or some other high-tech product, not running shoes or deodorant, doesn't mean you can't grab customers' imaginations. In fact, you have to. Having a new button or a faster processor won't win your marketing wars. To survive, a technology company must have a sword it can brandish, a flag it can wave, a set of values that its followers can look up to. A TechnoBrand, specifically designed for the attributes of technology buyers.

TechnoBrand your company and products and:

- Your people will become focused in the right areas because they will understand what customers care about and why they buy from you.
- Your marketing and advertising strategy will be on target and effective because you have the knowledge about your customers to make intelligent, well-founded decisions.

- Your brand, and hence your company's worth, will grow and prosper because you have invested in your brand equity.

Notes

1. Tod Johnson, "The Durability of Brands," *Advertising Research Foundation Executive Research Digest*, Feb. 28, 1991, 4.
2. Reed Abelson, "Brand Loyalty?" *SmartMoney,* January 1994, 88.
3. Alexandra Ourusoff, with Meenakshi Panchapakesan, "Who Says Brands Are Dead?" *Financial World*, Sept. 1, 1993, 40–50.
4. L. Ross Love, "Back to Basics: Up with Advertising," A.N.A. Advertising Issues Forum, San Francisco, Sept. 13–15, 1992.
5. Ed Vick, "Brands on Trial," *ADWEEK*, May 24, 1993, 24–31.
6. Kathleen Deveny, "Private Labels Whip Up More Optimism," *The Wall Street Journal*, Dec. 2, 1993, p. B8.
7. "Food Fundamentalism," *The Economist*, Dec. 4, 1993, 3–18.
8. Gary Levin, "'Price' Rises as Factor for Consumers," *Advertising Age*, Nov. 8, 1993, 37.
9. Tom Schmitz, "Tech Hits Prime Time," *San Jose Mercury News*, Feb. 23, 1992, p. 1E.
10. Michael Birkin, "Brand Valuation," in *Understanding Brands*, ed. Don Cowley (London: Kogan Page Limited, 1991).
11. Michael Birkin, "Brand Valuation," in *Understanding Brands*, ed. Don Cowley (London: Kogan Page Limited, 1991).
12. Laura Patterson, "Brand Building: Let the Chips Fly," *Upside*, October 1993, 93.

Index